T0145511

THE

WILD

GREAT

WALL

Phoneme Media
P.O. Box 411272
Los Angeles, CA 90041

ISBN: 978-1-944700-69-0

This book is distributed by Publishers Group West

Cover design and typesetting by Jaya Nicely
Cover Art by Yang Shang

Printed in the United States of America

Phoneme Media is a nonprofit media company dedicated to
promoting cross-cultural understanding, connecting people and
ideas through translated books and films.

http://phonememedia.org

THE

Zhu Zhu

WILD

Translated From the Chinese

GREAT

by Dong Li

WALL

PHONEME
MEDIA

目录

TABLE OF CONTENTS

IV (2012-)

IV (2012-)

I (1990-1999)

楼梯上

此刻楼梯上的男人数不胜数。
上楼,黑暗中已有肖邦。
下楼,在人群中孤寂地死亡。

Up the Stairs

This moment countless men up the stairs.
Upstairs, Chopin already in the dark.
Downstairs, dying alone in a crowd.

小镇的萨克斯

雨中的男人，有一圈细密的茸毛，
他们行走时像褐色的树，那么稀疏。
整条街道像粗大的萨克斯管伸过。

有一道光线沿着起伏的屋顶铺展，
雨丝落向孩子和狗。
树叶和墙壁上的灯无声地点燃。

我走进平原上的小镇，
镇上放着一篮果子。
我走到人的唇与萨克斯相触的门。

Small Town Saxophone

Men in rain, a halo of hair, thin and fine,
they walk like brown trees, so spread apart.
The street runs by like a large saxophone.

A line of light plays out along undulating roofs,
threads of rain fall upon children and dogs.
Leaves and wall lamps silently burn.

I walk into this small flatlands town,
a basket of chestnuts sits in town. I walk to the door
where human lips touch the saxophone.

厨房之歌

多么强大的风，
从对面的群山
吹拂到厨房里悬挂的围裙上，
屋脊像一块锈蚀的钟摆跟着晃动。

我们离街上的救护车
和山前的陵墓最远，
就像爱着围裙上绣着的牡丹，
我们爱着每一幅历史的彩图。

有水壶和几瓶酒，
水分被空气偷偷吸干的梨子，
还有谦恭地邻近水管的砧板。
在日光中，
厨房像野鸭梳理自己的羽毛。

厨房多么像它的主人，
或者他的爱人消失的手。
强大的风掀开了暗橱，
又把围裙吹倒在脚边。

刮除灶台边的污垢，
盒子被秋天打开的情欲也更亮了，
我们要更镇定地往枯草上撒盐，
将胡椒拌进睡眠。

强大的风
它有一些更特殊的金子
要交给首饰匠。
我们只管在饥饿的间歇里等待，
什么该接受，什么值得细细地描画。

The Kitchen Song

So strong a wind
blows from the facing mountain range
to the apron hanging in the kitchen,
the roof swings like a rusty pendulum.

We are farthest from the ambulance on the street
and the cemetery at the foot of the mountain.
Just as we love the peony-embroidered apron,
we love every colored illustration of history.

There is a kettle and a few bottles of wine,
a pear, its moisture sucked dry by the air,
and the cutting board that rests modestly
next to the water pipes. In the sunlight,
the kitchen combs its feathers like a wild duck.

The kitchen looks very much like its owner,
or his lover's vanishing hands.
Strong winds flip open cupboards
and blow the apron down at his feet.

The grime by the stove scraped,
the box of desire opened brighter by autumn,
we need to sprinkle salt more calmly on wilted grass
and stir pepper into sleep.

A powerful wind
brings a special kind of gold
to be given to the jewelry maker.
We wait merely in the respite between hungers,
for what to accept, what is worth a meticulous description.

沙滩

少于冬天的鸟。
少于记忆之外的日子。
少于我的影子；少于石头之中的
你的影子。

很少有这样的时刻，
我走过大风，也走过一下午的纬度
和海——语言，语言的尾巴
长满孔雀响亮的啼叫。

The Beach

Less than winter's bird.
Less than days outside memory.
Less than my shadow; less than
your shadow in rock.

This moment rare,
I walk through wind, through an afternoon's latitude
and the sea—language, tail of language
rife with the bright cries of a peacock.

我是弗朗索瓦·维庸

借你的戟一看，
巡夜人，
我是弗朗索瓦·维庸。
经午夜寻求
斜坡向阳的一侧，
我要在那里捉虱子，听低哑的滴水声。

这漫天的雪是我的奇痒，
巴黎像兽笼，在它的拱门，
全部的往事向外膨胀，
这是我的半首《烤鱼歌》，
赏一口酒如何？
某处门廊下停着一具女尸
你可以趁着微温行乐。

或者我教会你怎样掌管时间，
只要一把骰子
和金盆里几根香菜，
我还能摹拟暴风发出一阵嚎叫，
把烟囱里的火吹燃，
我的叔叔。

天堂里多热，
当天使抖落身上的羽毛，
我们的口涎却在嘴角结冰，
赏一口酒如何？
漫长的冬天，
一只狼寻找话语的森林。

I Am François Villon

Let me take a look at your halberd,
dear night watcher,
I am François Villon.
Past midnight, in search of
the sunlit side of a slanting slope,
where I want to catch lice, listen to hoarse drops of water.

The engulfing snow is my immense itch.
Paris like a cage, in its arch
the entire past expands outward.
This is my half -"Ballad of Grilling Fish,"
what about a sip of wine?
A lady's body rests on some porch,
you can entertain yourself while it is still warm.

Or I can teach you how to manage time
with only a handful of dice
and a few sprigs of parsley in the golden bowl.
I can mimic the howling of a storm
to rekindle the fire in the chimney,
my dear uncle.

It is so hot in heaven that
angels' feathers, slough down, yet
our saliva freezes to ice at the corners of our mouths.
What about a sip of wine?
Long, long winter,
a wolf looks for the forest of words.

和一位瑞典朋友在一起的日子

光不在玻璃上返回，
而是到来。
春天不是在冰雪上犹豫地停留，
等待动物爬出来，
河流随之柔软。
在南方的天空下，
阴影即使有厚度，
也是轻巧的一触，
就碎去。

水池上，
扁豆的睾丸
轻摇着，
轻摇着，
琉璃瓦的屋顶下
那些阴森的褶皱展开了。
人们一个接着一个，
穿过了街道
但又不知为什么穿过。

在"冰岛"
这样的词意味着的
北欧的孤寂里
（那里，每一座房屋
都是一个遥远的情人），
这里已经是盛夏，
这一天的人群
就是一个世纪里的人群。

Days With a Swedish Friend

Light does not return on the glass,
but arrives.
Spring does not linger on ice and snow,
waiting for the animals to come out.
Rivers then soften.
In the southern sky,
even if shadows have a certain thickness,
with a light touch,
they break.

On the pond,
the testicles of hyacinth beans
rock softly,
rock softly.
Under the glazed roof
dark creases unfold.
One by one, people
cross streets
not yet knowing why they cross.

In "ice-land,"
where such a word means
the loneliness of Scandinavia
(there, every house
is a faraway lover),
it is already midsummer.
The crowd of this day
is the crowd of this century.

光还在增强。
杨柳像溅起来的池水吞没我们
和你手中的
鱼眼镜头。
黑极了的煤可以做镜子了。
蝴蝶轻盈得可以反过来承担什么了；
蝴蝶开始展翅——
不再要求你盛放
干涩的卵。

我将手放在你
那正在熔化的雕像式的躯体上，
你不是流亡者
而是选择了另一种生活，
但是你说："流亡有很多种……"

Light intensifies.
Like water splashed from the pond, willows devour us
and the fisheye lens
in your hand.
Embers, when dark enough, can be used as mirrors.
Butterflies are so light that they can take something on instead;
butterflies begin to flutter their wings—
and no longer ask you to hold
their parched eggs.

I put my hand
on your statue-like body, now melting.
You are not an exile
but have chosen another way of life,
and you say: "There are many kinds of exile…"

II (2000-2005)

林中空地

我获得的是一种被处决后的安宁，头颅撂在一边。

周围，同情的屋顶成排，它们彼此紧挨着。小镇居民们的身影一掠而过，只有等它们没入了深巷，才会发出议论的啼声。

Clearing in the Woods

I gain peace, peace after execution, head left to one side.

Sympathetic roofs line up around me, leaning close against each other. The shadows of villagers flit past, and only after they disappear into deep alleys do heated cries arise.

青烟

I

清澈的刘海;
发髻盘卷,
一个标准的小妇人。
她那张椭圆的脸,像一只提前
报答了气候的水蜜桃。

跷起腿,半转身躯,一只手肘撑在小桌子上,
手指夹住一支燃烧的香烟(烟燃尽,
有人会替她续上一支,再走开)。在屋中
她必须保持她的姿势至终,
摄影师走来走去,画家盯住自己的画布,
一只苍蝇想穿透玻璃飞出,最后看得她想吐。

晚上她用一条包满冰的毛巾敷住手臂。

II

第二天接着干。又坐在
小圆凳上,点起烟。画家
和她低声交谈了几句,问她的祖籍、姓名。
摄影师没有来,也许不来了?
透过画家背后的窗,可以望见外滩。
江水打着木桩。一艘单桅船驶向对岸荒岛上。

Blue Smoke

I

Clear bangs,
a coiled bun,
a standard little lady.
Her oval face looks like a peach that repays
the climate before its time.

She crosses her legs, turns her body halfway around, an elbow on
    a small table,
a burning cigarette between her fingers (once the cigarette is finished,
someone will hand her another one and then walk away). In the room
she must maintain her posture until the end.
A photographer walks back and forth, a painter stares at his canvas,
a fly wants to fly through the glass. She watches and wants to vomit.

At night, she wraps her arms with a towel full of ice.

II

They continue to work the next day. She sits back down
on the small round stool and lights a cigarette. The painter
talks to her briefly in a low voice, and asks where she comes from
    and her name.
The photographer has not come yet, perhaps he will not come?
Through the window behind the painter's back, she can see the Bund.
    The river
beats upon wooden poles. A sloop sails toward the deserted island
    on the other shore.

一辆电车在黄包车铃声里掣过。她
想起冠生园软软的座垫，想着自己
不够浑圆的屁股，在上边翘得和黑女人一样高。
这时她忘记了自己被画着，往常般吸一口烟，

烟圈徐徐被吐出。
被挡在画架后面的什么哐啷地一声。
画家黑黝黝的眼窝再次对准了她，吓了
她一跳。她低下头扯平
已经往上翻卷到大腿根的旗袍。
这一天过得快多了。

III

此后几天她感觉自己
不必盛满她的那个姿势，或者
完全就让它空着。

她坐在那里，好像套着一层
表情的模壳，薄薄的，和那件青花旗袍一样。
在模壳的里边——
她已经在逛街，已经
懒洋洋地躺在了一张长榻上分开了双腿
大声的打呵欠，已经
奔跑在天边映黄了溪流的油菜田里。

摄影师又出现过一次。
把粗壮奇长的镜头伸出
皮革机身，近得几乎压在她脸上，
她顺势给他一个微笑，甜甜的。

A trolley rushes by in the ringing of the rickshaw bell. She
thinks of soft cushions at Guan Sheng Yuan, thinks of her bottom
that is not round enough, not as bubble-like as a black lady's.
Now she forgets that she is being painted, and continues to smoke,

rings of smoke slowly spit out.
Something behind the easel bangs on the ground.
The painter's shady eye sockets scrutinize her again and that startles
her. She lowers her head, while smoothing over
the cheongsam that has already curled up the deep of her thighs.
Today it goes by much faster.

III

The next few days she feels
that she does not have to be fully present in her posture, or
to be completely inattentive.

She sits there, as if wrapped
in a thin mask of expression, thin as her blue-and-white cheongsam.
Inside the mask—
she already wanders the streets, already
lies lazily on a long couch and parts her legs,
yawning in a loud voice, already
runs by the sky's edge in the canola fields that yellow the streams.

The photographer appears once again.
The thick and unbelievably long lens pokes out
of the leathered body, so close that it presses against her face,
she yields and smiles him a sweet smile.

一台电唱机:
"蔷薇蔷薇处处开";
永春和派人送来 陪伴他们的工作。

IV

她开始跑出那个模壳,
站到画家的身边打量那幅画:
画中人既像又不像她,
他在她的面颊上涂抹了太多的胭脂,
夹烟的手画得过于纤细,
他画的乳房是躲在绸衣背后而不是从那里鼓胀,
并且,他把她背影里的墙
画成一座古怪的大瀑布
僵立着但不流动。
唯独从她手指间冒起的一缕烟
真的很像在那里飘,在空气中飘。

她还发现这个画家
其实很早就画完了这幅画,
在后来很长的一段日子里,每天
他只是在不停地涂抹那缕烟。

A record player plays
"Rose Rose Blossoms Everywhere";
Yong Chun He sends someone over to keep them company.

IV

She begins to escape from the mask,
and stands by the painter to see the painting:
the lady in the painting does and doesn't look like her,
he puts too much make-up on her face,
the hand that holds the cigarette too delicate,
the painted breasts hide instead of bulging beneath her silk clothes,
and he paints the wall in her shadow
as a strange waterfall,
stiff and static.
Only a wisp of smoke rising from between her fingers
looks as if it truly floats, floating in the air.

She also discovers that this painter
has in fact long finished the painting,
and during the long days since, every day
he does nothing but fiddle with that wisp of smoke.

Note: Guan Sheng Yuan was a famous shop in Shanghai that sold homemade snacks.
    "Rose Rose Blossoms Everywhere" was a jazz song popular on the Bund in
    Shanghai during the 1930s.
    Yong Chun He was the tobacco company that hired a prostitute as their
    advertising model.

野长城

I

地球表面的标签
或记忆深处的一道勒痕，消褪在
受风沙和干旱的侵蚀
而与我们的肤色更加相似的群山。

我们曾经在这边。即使
是一位征召自小村镇的年轻士兵，
也会以直立的姿势与富有者的心情
透过箭垛打量着外族人，
那群不过是爬行在荒原上的野兽。

在这边，我们已经营造出一只巨大的浴缸，
我们的日常是一种温暖而慵倦的漫泡。
当女人们在花园里荡秋千，
男人们的目光嗜好于从水中找到倒影；

带血的、未煮熟的肉太粗俗了，
我们文明的屋檐
已经精确到最后那一小截的弯翘。

II

现在，经历着
所有的摧毁中最彻底的一种：
遗忘——它就像

The Wild Great Wall

I

Label of the Earth's surface
or a trace strangled deep in memory
vanishes at the invasion of sandstorms and droughts
into mountains whose skin tone is ever closer to ours.

We were once here. Even
a young solider conscripted from a small town
would stand tall and with the heart of a rich man
judge aliens through piles of arrows, the herd of people,
no better than beasts crawling through a wasteland.

Here, we have already built a giant bathtub
to soak ourselves in warm, languid routine.
While women play on a swing in the garden,
men's eyes seek out reflections in the water;

bloody, barely-cooked meat too uncouth,
the eaves of our civilization
are now demanding to the last stretch of their upward tips.

II

Now, go through
the most thorough of all destructions:
forgetting—it is like

一头爬行动物的脊椎
正进入风化的尾声，
山脊充满了侏罗纪的沉寂，
随着落日的遥远马达渐渐地平息，
余晖像锈蚀的箭镞坠落。

我来追溯一种在我们出生前就消失的生活，
如同考据学的手指苦恼地敲击
一只空壳的边沿，
它的内部已经掏干了。

III

在陡坡的那几棵桃树上，
蜜蜂们哼着歌来回忙碌着，
它们选择附近的几座
就像摔破的陶罐般的烽火台
做为宿营地。

那歌词的大意仿佛是：
一切都还给自然……

野草如同大地深处的手指，
如同蓬勃的、高举矛戟的幽灵部队
登上了坍塌的台阶，
这样的时辰，无数受惊的风景
一定正从各地博物馆的墙壁上仓惶地逃散。

a reptile spine
moving toward its final decay.
Mountain ridges beam in Jurassic quietude,
as the sun sets, the engine dies slowly down.
The remnant light falls like rusty arrows.

I come to trace the life that disappeared long before our birth,
as if the philological fingers knock
the ridge of an empty shell,
whose inside has been picked clean, in anguish.

III

In the peach trees on the steep slope,
bees hum and buzz around.
They have set up a campsite
in a nearby beacon tower
that has been smashed like earthenware.

Their song seems to say:
everything returns to nature…

Wild grass, like fingers deep in the earth,
like a fiery troop of ghosts with halberds and lances held high,
climbs onto collapsed steps.
This moment, countless startled landscapes must be fluttering
and fleeing off the walls in museums everywhere.

小城

一切只是整齐和美，
奢侈，平静和欢乐迷醉。
　　——夏尔·波德莱尔《邀游》

I

当我在早晨的窗前
喝着咖啡，眼前是旅馆的

大花园，鲜花盛开，
灌木丛被修剪得平整；

在一条砾石的小径旁
矗立着一尊半裸的女神，

在我周围是低低交谈的人声，
他们优雅的举止，酷似

桌上的玻璃器皿
和反光的银器。

II

老港湾里停满游艇，
松垂在桅杆上的绳索如同琴弦，

等待被绷紧、被更迅猛的风弹奏——
沿岸咖啡馆的大多数桌子还空着；

Small Town

I

Early in the morning before the window I
drink coffee, before my eyes: the hotel's

big garden, flowers in bloom,
bushes trimmed even;

beside a gravel footpath
stands a statue of a half-naked goddess.

Around me, soft murmurs of people talking,
their elegant manners closely resemble

glassware on the table
and reflective silverware.

II

Moored yachts fill the old harbor.
Ropes slack on the mast as if strings

waiting to be tightened, to be plucked violently by the wind—
most tables in cafés along the shore are still empty;

成千上万的游人们，
他们将会在夏天到来。

当我沿着松林走向
海滩，经过那些别墅

和那座大公园——
寒冷而清旷的空气里

有一种空虚
不同于贫困与绝望的滋味，

很像一座铺满天鹅绒的监狱，
或者是显贵们居住的带喷泉的医院。

III

夜深时我独自在城中闲逛，
循着乐曲声找到一家酒吧，

将自己淹没在
啤酒的金色泡沫里，

而在我沮丧的大脑深处
波德莱尔的诗句好像咒语

始终在盘旋，好像我
就是他，在航行的半途

受困于毛里求斯的港湾之夜，
听见丛林深处抽打奴隶的鞭子

thousands of tourists
will come here in summertime.

When I walk along the pine forest
to the beach, past those mansions

and a big park—
in the cold, clean air

there is a void
distinct from the taste of poverty and despair,

more like a velvet-carpeted prison or a hospital
with a fountain where the privileged stay.

III

Late night I stroll alone through the city
and find a bar by its music

and sink myself
in the golden foam of beer,

deep in my dejected mind
Baudelaire's verse

lingers like a curse, still, as if I
were him, halfway through the voyage,

a night stuck in the bay of Mauritius,
listening to slaves whipped in the deep forest,

就像我往昔写下的诗篇
回响在自己的面颊。

IV

是不是一个人走得太远时，
就想回头捡拾他的姓名、

家史，和破朽的摇篮？
是不是他讨厌影子的尾随

而一旦它消失，
自由就意味着虚无？

是否我已经扭曲
如一根生锈的弹簧，

彻底丧失了弹性？
是否在彻底的黑暗中

我才感觉到实存？
正如飓风与骇浪，

尖利的暗礁
和恐怖的旋涡，

反倒带给水手将一生
稳稳地揣入怀中的感受。

as if my poems written in the past
echo in my face.

IV

Is it that when a man walks too far,
he wants to return to pick up his name,

family history, and the broken-down cradle?
Is it that he hates being trailed by shadows,

and once they are gone,
freedom means ennui?

Isn't it that I am already twisted
like a rusty spring,

its elasticity lost?
Isn't it that only in complete darkness

can I feel the truth of existence?
Like whirlwinds or engulfing torrents,

sharp hidden reefs
and terrifying swirls of water

bring to sailors the feeling, instead,
of having a life squarely held in their arms.

V

我的记忆沉重，转瞬间
就能使嘴唇变成泥土，

我的爱粘滞，像一条
割不断的脐带——

我的欢乐是悬崖上易朽的绳栏，
我的风景是一个古老的深渊。

难眠于这子夜的旅馆，
推开窗户吮吸着

冰冷的海风，我渴望归期
一如当初渴望启程，

我们的一生
就是桃花源和它的敌人。

V

My memory heavy, able, in a split second
to turn lips to mud,

my love sticky, like an
unbreakable umbilical cord—

my happiness, a decaying rope railing on a cliff,
my landscape, an ancient abyss.

Unable to sleep in this midnight hotel,
I open the window to suck

on the ice-cold sea wind. I long to return
—as I longed for the first sail.

Our entire life is
the peach blossom spring and its foe.

III (2006-2011)

爬墙虎

她是疯狂的，柔软的手掌
已经蜕变成虎爪和吸盘，
从最初的一跃开始，覆盖，
层层叠叠，吞没整面墙，缝合
整个屋子，黯淡下全部光线；
从不退缩，即使步入了虚空
也会变成一队螺旋形的盾牌；
即使入冬后枝叶全部枯萎，仍然
用缝纫线被抽走后留下的成串针孔
镶嵌自己的身形；她有僵持的决心，
被粉碎的快感，和春天到来时
那一份膨胀的自我犒劳，如同
在沙盘里插上密密的小旗，
如同蜂拥的浪尖以为扎破了礁岩；
她是绝望的，无法进入到屋中，
但她至少遮蔽了外面的一切，
年复一年，她是真的在爱着。

The Creeper

She runs wild, soft palms
now morphed to tiger claws and suckers,
which, from the first leap cover,
overlay, devour the whole wall, stitch up
the whole room, dim all the lights;
she never backs off; even if stepping into a void
will turn her into a shield of corkscrews;
even if all her leaves wilt in winter, she still
decorates her body with a string of holes,
once the sewn threads are pulled out; her tenacity
holds up in a stalemate, she takes pleasure in being
crushed, and her self-congratulation expands in the spring
like tightly-spaced pennants stuck in a sandbox,
as if thorny waves think they have slit the shoal;
she despairs, unable to enter the room,
but at least she camouflages everything outside:
year after year, she truly loves.

石窟

落日无法追赶，
我们到达时天已经暗去。
地轴吱嘎的转动声响彻在两岸之间，
整条河好像被埋进幽深的洞穴，
只能隔着悬浮的地平线倾听。

旅馆在山顶——
一条曾经萦回在白居易暮年的山道，
积满了无法再回到枝头的落叶；
在旅馆的登记簿上，
我们的一生被判决为外乡人。

眺望对岸的旧栏杆也在山顶；
能看见什么？泼墨的长卷不留星点的空白，
风如挽联般飘卷，惟有越织越厚的雾
从高空垂落，可以切割成枕头、床和被单，
充填在空荡如我们头脑般的房间。

黑鸟的翅膀惊起在檐头，犬吠
来自山脚的村庄；尽管关上了窗户，
仍然能够听见低吼的潮水
一浪接着一浪，就像靠岸的独木筏
催促着我们立刻出发——

今夜我们不过河，
临睡前我们仍旧打开电视，
像灯蛾依偎在冰冷、颤动的荧光，
我们宁愿石窟继续风化在对岸的夜幕深处，
一如整个历史都安睡在大自然的陵寝里。

The Grotto

Unable to chase the setting sun,
it is dark when we arrive.
The earth's turning axis squeaks between the banks.
The river seems buried in a deep cave,
only audible over the hovering horizon.

The hotel sits atop the hill—
a lane that once wound through Bai Juyi's old age
is piled with leaves unable to return to their branches;
in the hotel registration book,
we are condemned as aliens.

Watch the old railings on the other bank atop the hill;
what is there to see? The long ink-splashed scroll shows no spot
    of white,
wind unrolls like an elegiac couplet, only the fog weaves thicker,
falling straight from the sky, cut into pillows, sheets, and quilts,
filling up a room that is empty like our mind.

A blackbird startles on the eaves, dogs bark
from the village at the foot of the hill; though windows are closed,
the roaring tides can still be heard,
wave after wave, as if a raft pulled to shore
urges us to set off now—

tonight we cannot cross the river.
At bedtime we still turn on the TV,
like moths leaning into the cold, trembling fluorescent light.
We would prefer that the grotto weather deep at night on the far bank,
like history asleep in nature's tomb.

河流标明一条心理的界线，
我们害怕地狱般的血腥和腐朽一起复活，
自己像棋盘上的卒子再无回返的机会——
却又在梦中端起微弱的烛台，走上石阶，
去瞻详遥远的黄金时代。

The river marks the limit of the psyche.
We fear that the purgatorial blood and decay might come back
    to life and
that we ourselves like pawns on the chessboard can no longer
    return—
but in a dream raise a candelabra, walk up the stairs,
and scrutinize a distant golden age.

Note: Bai Juyi was a Tang dynasty poet.

寄北

我梦见一街之隔有家洗衣店，
成群的洗衣机发出一阵阵低吼。
透过形同潜望镜的玻璃圆孔，
能看见不洁的衣物在经受酷刑，
它们被吸入机筒腹部的漩涡，
被吞噬、缠绕，来回翻滚于急流，
然后藻草般软垂，长长的纤维
在涌来的清水里漂浮，逐渐透明；
有一股异样的温暖从内部烘烤，
直到它皱缩如婴儿，在梦中蜷伏。
那里，我脱下那沾满灰尘的外套后
赤裸着，被投放到另一场荡涤，
亲吻和欢爱，如同一簇长满
现实的尖刺并且携带风疹的荨麻
跳动在火焰之中；我们消耗着
空气，并且只要有空气就足够了。
每一次，你就是那洗濯我的火苗，
而我就是那件传说中的火浣衫。

To the North

I dream of the laundromat a street away.
Herds of washing machines roar and growl.
Through the bathyscopic view of a porthole,
soiled clothes are tortured,
as they are sucked into the swirl of the machine's belly,
devoured and snarled, twisting in torrents of water,
then sagging like sea grass, long fibers afloat
in surges of clear water, turning more transparent;
an uncanny warmth bakes within,
until it crimps like a baby curled up in sleep.
There, after taking off my dusty overcoat,
naked, I am thrown into another wash,
kissing and lovemaking, like a bush full
of reality's thorns and marked by nettle rash
sizzling in the flame; we consume
air, and having just air is enough.
Each spin, you are the flames that wash me,
and I am the asbestos shirt of legend.

海岛

有生孰不在岛上？
　　——苏轼

放逐，这就是对权力说真话的结果，
但也不必过于美化他，将他的政治头脑
看得和他的诗人头脑一样发达，
给他一个国家，他终究不脱独裁的窠臼。

现在他已抵达了这个国家的南极，
或者是抵达了若干个世纪之后的今天
一个诗人的位置：被彻底地边缘化，
好像黄昏时空荡的海滨浴场上

被遗留在桌上的收音机。大陆
像收起了吊桥的城市远在海的另一边，
群山般环抱的潮水，退去如雪崩般
无情，只留下泡沫、珊瑚和成堆的垃圾。

他栽种竹子如同戍边的将士带来了
情人的青丝，在米酒中酿造江南，
他读陶渊明，在这里读就像有
一架天文望远镜猛然将猎户星推入心扉。

小路在村外连接起荒寂，贫乏，瘴疠。
酷热，足以烧熔棚顶和心智。
惟有月亮感恩于他不朽的赞颂，
频频来访，在长夜里治疗他的失忆。

Island in the Sea

Who was not born on an island?
   —Su Shi

Exile: the outcome of telling the truth before authority.
But there is no need to idealize him and assume his political wits
are as developed as his poetic faculty.
Given a country, he would never slip the despot's trap.

Now he reaches the southern extreme of this country,
or centuries after his time reaches today,
a poet's place: completely marginalized,
like a radio left on a table at twilight

on an empty beach. The continent sits
far across the sea, like a suspension bridge drawn up.
Waves, like embracing mountains, ebb like an avalanche
of ruthless snow, leaving behind foam, coral, and banks of trash.

He plants bamboo as if soldiers on the frontier bringing in
locks of lovers' hair, brews South-of-Yangtze in rice wine,
and reads Tao Yuanming, reading him here like having
a telescope push Orion out of the blue and into the heart.

A lane outside the village links desolation, poverty, and malaria.
The overbearing heat is enough to melt down the shed's metal and
   psyche.
Only the moon is grateful for his immortal praise
and visits often, healing his memory loss during the long night.

噢，他必须收起鲁宾逊的傲慢，
在异化的环境里重新定调。
他必须振作精神，不扮演文明的遗老，
不做词语的幽灵，不卖弄苦难，

而只是澄清生命的原址——
以它为一种比例尺，重新丈量大陆，
绘下新的世界地图，或者
像沙鸥一无所负，自在地滑翔。

Ah, he must put away Crusoe's arrogance
and find new tones in the alien environment.
He must cheer himself up, not act like civilization's castaway,
not become a ghost, not traffic in suffering,

but clarify life's wellspring—
and use it as a scale to remeasure the land
and draw a map of the new world, or
like a seagull, carry nothing and glide carefree.

Note: Tao Yuanming was a poet from the Six Dynasties period, a foremost
representative of Chinese landscape poetry.

内陆

夜晚如此荒凉，要用十几座村镇的灯火
才能照亮一幅眼前的地图。这里，
炉灶是寂寞的，炊烟仅仅升起一种尊严。
干涸的大河里流动着沙，就像
一千种方言述说单调和停滞——
当我攥住地图的一角，远处的大都市
就像从松开了绳子的手中飘散到海边的
大串气球，眼前这些古老的地名
要求我认领，说它们属于我，
早在我出生之前，血液中就涌动着它们的回声——
它们来自同一个被遣散的家园，
穿过落日的针孔，遍野而来，
要求我成为一座收容所，一只未来的漂流瓶。

Inland

Night so desolate, it takes the lamps and fires of a dozen villages
to light up a map before the eyes. Here,
the stove is lonely, cooking smoke raises only a wisp of dignity.
In the big dried-up river sands drift,
like a thousand dialects telling of monotony and stasis—
when I grip a corner of the map, the faraway cities
are swept seaward like balloons in a cluster from a hand
that has loosened its grip on their strings. Ancient names before me
demand my recognition, telling me that they belong to me.
Before I was born, their echoes rumbled in my blood—
they come from the same cast-off homeland,
through the needle eye of the setting sun, across the wild,
asking me to become a shelter, a floating bottle of morrow.

江南共和国

——柳如是墓前

I

裁缝送来了那件朱红色的大氅，
它有雪白的羊毛翻领，帽商
送来了皮质斗笠，鞋店送来长筒靴。
门外，一匹纯黑的马备好了鞍——

我盛装，端坐在镜中，就像
即将登台的花旦，我饰演昭君，
那个出塞的人质，那个在政治的交媾里
为国家赢得喘息机会的新娘。

已是初夏，冰雪埋放在地窖中，
在往年，槐花也已经酿成了蜜。
此刻城中寂寂地，所有的城门紧闭，
只听见江潮在涌动中播放对岸的马蹄。

我盛装，将自己打扮成一个典故，
将美色搅拌进寓言，我要穿越全城，
我要走上城墙，我要打马于最前沿的江滩，
为了去激发涣散的军心。

II

我爱看那些年轻的军士们
长着绒毛的嘴唇，他们的眼神
羞怯而直白，吞咽的欲望
沿着粗大的喉结滚动，令胸膛充血，

South-of-Yangtze, a Republic

—Before the Grave of Liu Rushi

I

The tailor brings in the vermillion cloak,
which has a snow-white turned-out collar of fleece. The hatter
brings in a leather rain hat. The cobbler brings in high boots.
Out the door, a night-black horse is already saddled—

I am dressed in my Sunday best, sitting in the mirror, like
a vivacious young lady about to take the stage, in the role of Zhaojun,
the hostage who crossed the border, the bride to political copulation
who won her country a moment of breath.

Now early summer, snow and ice are buried in the cellar,
locust blossoms of bygone years have been made into honey.
This moment the city quiet, all its gates shut tight,
only the river's rolling tide broadcasts hoof beats from the other bank.

I am dressed in my Sunday best, dressed as a literary allusion,
blending allure with parable. I want to cross the city.
I want to climb its walls. I want to ride horseback to the riverfront
to rouse our demoralized troops.

II

I love watching those young soldiers
with their downy lips. The look in their eyes
shy yet direct, their hemming and hawing desires bob
alongside their large Adam's apples, above their blood-swelled chests.

他们远胜过我身边那些遗老，
那些乔装成高士的怨妇，
捻着天道的人质计算着个人的得失，
在大敌面前，如同在床上很快就败下阵来。

哦，我是压抑的
如同在垂老的典狱长怀抱里
长久得不到满足的妻子，借故走进
监狱的围墙内，到犯人们贪婪的目光里攫获快感，

而在我内心的深处还有
一层不敢明言的晦暗幻象
就像布伦城的妇女们期待破城的日子，
哦，腐朽糜烂的生活，它需要外部而来的重重一戳。

III

薄暮我回家，在剔亮的灯芯下，
我以那些纤微巧妙的词语，
就像以建筑物的倒影在水上
重建一座文明的七宝楼台，

再一次，骄傲和宁静
荡漾在内心，我相信
有一种深邃无法被征服，它就像
一种阴道，反过来吞噬最为强悍的男人。

我相信每一次重创、每一次打击
都是过境的飓风，然后
还将是一枝桃花摇曳在晴朗的半空，
潭水倒映苍天，琵琶声传自深巷。

They are far better than these holdovers around me,
these complaining ladies who pass for honorable men,
rubbing heavenly beads to tally their own loss and gain,
before the enemy, as in bed, soon pulling back from the fray.

Alas, I feel repressed,
like the long dissatisfied wife in the arms
of an old warden, who enters the walled yard on some made-up
    pretense
and harvests pleasures from the inmates' hungry gazes.

But deep in my heart there is
an obscure illusion that I dare not speak of,
like when the women of Boulogne eagerly waited to be conquered.
Alas, decadent life — it needs a hard thrust from the outside.

III

At dusk I come home, by the light of a lamp with a trimmed wick
I use smart, delicate words
to rebuild the godly pagoda of humanism
on the reflection of an edifice in the water.

Once again, pride and tranquility
ripple through my heart and I believe
there is a depth that cannot be conquered. It is like
a vagina that can swallow even the most virile men.

I believe that every deep wound and every hard blow
is a passing whirlwind, and afterward
peach flowers still waver in clear midair,
a pond reflects the vast sky, the sound of the pipa rumbles from
    deep alleys.

Note: Liu Rushi was a Chinese courtesan and poet in the late Ming dynasty.
    Zhaojun was known as one of the Four Beauties of ancient China.
    A Pipa is a four-string Chinese musical instrument.

乍暖还寒

一夜间山岭又白了头。
坍塌在郊外古道边的亭子
意味着即使在两三个知己之间
也不再有相宜的小气候了。

才吐出新芽的柳丝
重新被裹上封蜡，
梅花捻灭了灯芯，
鱼在湖中游成了化石——

风筝绕缠在老树的卷轴上，
生活，还是那张旧底片……
我们从衣橱里翻寻出冬装，
如同假释的犯人重新领回囚服；

我们就像渐成人形的陶土，
在炉窑冷去的灰烬里烧到一半。
这究竟是一部怎样的历法——
规定了我们的一生总在乍暖还寒之间？

Cold Front

A ridge whitens its head again overnight.
Outside a city, a pavilion crumbling by the ancient route
seems to say that even between two or three friends
that spot of pleasant weather cannot last.

Willows newly decked in wispy green
are now sealed in wax again,
plum blossoms nip the wick,
fish swim into fossils in the lake—

a kite tangles itself on the scroll-peg of an old tree,
life, still that undeveloped negative...
we dig out winter coats from the wardrobe,
like paroled prisoners getting back their striped garb;

like clay, we slowly take on human shape, half burned
in the ashes now cooling in the kiln.
What on earth is this calendar
that dictates that our life stays on the cold front?

旧上海

　　—给S.T.

狂欢节，我们的青春赶上了末班车。
海关大楼的钟已经更换机芯，
它的指针转动整个城市。晨雾里
汽笛齐鸣，佝偻的外滩已经卸掉刑枷，
伸直的爱奥尼亚柱在水中重现殖民时代的倒影。
别错过观看八点以前大街上的人潮，
飞奔的亿万蚁足抬走一个谎言。每一天
都是新的，都是万花筒里的七彩图形，
你站着而奇遇在涌向你。噢，太多的盲点
就像老石库门里暗湿的、布满窟窿的窗，
在移去了阴霾的日子里排队等待曝光。

两座大学之间隔着一座铁路桥，你读文学
而我读法律，无论我们在学习什么，
都是在学习呼吸自由。当一部
未竟的忏悔录躺在医院里接受瞻仰，
一座地下图书馆在迅速扩大：尼采，佛洛伊德，
萨特和亲爱的提奥……那时全城的精英们
能够孵化有血有肉的蛋，补丁和假领
映衬着灵魂，诗歌是高尚或卑鄙的通行证，
通往友谊和梦想，也通往自我分裂、垃圾堆、
和权力通奸的床，直到最后的夏天来临。

Old Shanghai

—For S.T.

A carnival, our youth catches the last train.
The customs tower clock has gotten a new set of gears,
its minute hand turns the whole city around. In the morning fog
whistles blast in unison, the hunched-over Bund casts off its shackles,
the colonial age returns in the reflections on the water of tall ionic
    columns.
Don't miss watching the crowd on the street before eight o'clock.
Millions of ants carry away a lie. Every day
is new, a jigsaw puzzle in the kaleidoscope.
You stand and adventures surge toward you. Ah, too many blind spots,
like a Shikumen-style façade, dim and damp and full of holes,
line up to be exposed once these overcast days have filed by.

Two universities separated by a railway bridge, you study literature
and I study law, whatever we are learning,
we are learning to breathe freedom. While an
unfinished confession lies in the hospital and accepts admiration,
an underground library expands quickly: Nietzsche, Freud,
Sartre, and dear Theo…by which time all of the city's elites
can brood on eggs of flesh and blood, patches and detachable collars
betoken the soul, poetry is a pass for the despicable and the noble,
toward friendship and dream, toward schizophrenia and trash
and the adulterous bed of power, until the eventual arrival of summer.

一场精神的狂欢猝然地中断，
我们收拾行李，感觉它比来时更轻，
就像摁在食指下的一声轻嘘；当
推土机铲平了记忆的地平线，当生活的
航线再也难以交叉，当我们的姑娘们
早已经成为母亲，当上海已经变成纽约，
二十年间我越来越少地到来，每一次
都几乎认不出它——我们怎能料到
你每夜都潜回那隐埋的雷区，来擦拭
遗像的镜框，来挥舞堂吉诃德的长矛？

你入炼狱，将我们全部禁锢在外边。

A spiritual carnival breaks off abruptly.
I pack my luggage and feel that it is lighter than before,
like a whimper pressed under the index finger; as bulldozers
level the horizon of memory, as life's
sails will not overlap for good, as our girls
turn into mothers, as Shanghai becomes New York City,
for the past twenty years, I have been here less and less.
On each visit I hardly recognize it—how would we know that
each night you sneak back through hidden minefields, to wipe off
the portrait frames of the dead, to brandish Don Quixote's long
    lance?

You enter purgatory and bar all of us out.

多伦路

蚌壳般灰冷的天空下
成排的红砖老建筑。街边，
一家放映默片的咖啡馆门前，
女模特身穿旗袍，为下期
时尚杂志的封面走动在镜头中——
这城市经常有回到那个年代的需要。

邻近的街区里有一座小楼，
仿佛依旧满屋子的烟雾和咳嗽……
在窗边一张斑驳的大桌子上，他
用手术刀般的笔尖，剖开
老中国的胸膛，检查它的肝胆，
它的肺，它的胃和呼吸道——

然后，洗手，下楼，接受
年轻妻子和门徒们敬畏的注视；
晚餐时他抨击他的同行和病人，
抨击所有脆弱、多情的物种。
他有意以一己之力振兴民族版画业，
要求它们酷似珂勒惠支……
（私下里他喜欢比亚兹莱）。

他也抨击四周那围合的租界，
抹着口红的霓虹灯吞噬着
来开洋荤的乡下财主；
到处是穿旗袍的商女，和
以爵士乐来演奏的《后庭花》，
娱乐的分贝盖过了祥林嫂的啜泣，
革命党人的演讲，和越来越近的枪声。

Duolun Road

Under a sky cold and gray like a clamshell
are rows of old red brick buildings. By the street corner,
in front of a café that shows silent films,
a female model wears a cheongsam and poses
before a lens for the next month's cover—
often this city feels the need to return to that time.

There was a small building on the nearby block
that still looks full of smoke and coughs…
on a large motley table by the window, he
used a scalpel-like nib, to open
old China's chest, to check its liver and gallbladder,
its lungs, its stomach and respiratory tract—

then he washed his hands, went downstairs and accepted
the reverent gaze of his young wife and disciples;
during dinner he attacked his peers and patients,
attacked all those frail, maudlin creatures. He planned
to revive the nation's woodcut business on his own
and asked that the works look like Kollwitz's…
(in private he liked Beardsley).

He also attacked the surrounding foreign concessions.
Lipstick-wearing neon lights engulfed country moneybags
who came to taste foreign titillations; business ladies
in cheongsam and "Tune of Backyard Flowers"
played in a jazz style were everywhere. Decibels
of amusement overshadowed Xianglin Sao's sobs,
revolutionary speeches and approaching gunshots.

他的嗓音冷，硬，逐一宣布
每种器官、每根神经，和每种
希望的垂亡，宣布整个旧大陆
是一座燃烧的铁屋，是一座
海啸时瘟疫也在蔓延的孤岛；
不要叫醒任何一个人，
因为已经无路可逃……

他该庆幸自己没有活到
世纪的下半叶，等待他的
"要么是闭嘴要么是坐牢"，不，
即使闭嘴也难逃铁窗的厄运，而且
是和他一个也不打算宽恕的那些人
一起，被批斗被侮辱……他

往日的好斗不过像一场游戏，
而他意识到自己的缺点已经晚了——
面对相同的命运，道歉已变得多余。
假如他能够幸存，一定是在这现世的
拔舌地狱深处，强忍住肋骨
被踢断的疼痛，弓身打扫着厕所；但

也许他仍旧一个也不打算宽恕，
因为终其一生他都无法走出那一天——
那堂在仙台医校观看幻灯片的解剖课，
从那天起他感觉自己像布鲁诺
被扔进了火刑堆中，肉体毁灭过一次
而道德感垂直起飞，兀鹫般追猎腐臭；
他焦灼的眼已经看不见更多。

Cold, stiff, his voice pointed out
every organ, every nerve, and every imminent death
of hope, stating that the entire old continent
was a burning iron house, was a
lone island beset by plagues and tsunami;
don't wake anybody up,
there's no escape…

he should have been glad that he had not survived
into the latter half of the century, for what awaited him
was *either shut up or go to jail*, no, even if his mouth
had been shut, he could not have escaped prison, and
together with those he never intended to forgive,
to be denounced and insulted…his

combative days were no more than a game,
when he realized his flaws it would have been too late—
in the face of shared fate, apologies were of little use.
Had he survived, it would have been in the deep
of a living hell where tongues were ripped out, he would have borne
the pain of ribs being kicked, cleaned toilets with a hunchback; but

perhaps he would still never forgive anyone,
because to the very end he could not emerge from that day—
when those slides were shown during the anatomy lesson
at Sendai Medical School, from that day on, he felt himself
like Giordano Bruno thrown to death on a pyre, life's flesh destroyed,
morals flying straight up, like a vulture chasing after the rancid;
there was nothing his charred eyes could still see.

Note: "Tune of Backyard Flowers" is an ancient tune that usually alludes to the decline
of a dynasty.

Xianglin Sao—a character from a story by Lu Xun—was a young widow forced by
her in-laws to marry an old man. After the old man died she returned to her in-laws and
became mentally ill due to harsh treatment.

Lu Xun resolved to become a writer after his anatomy professor at Sendai Medical
School showed slides of Chinese citizens executed by Japanese colonial authorities in
Qingdao, China.

先驱

他们当中有一个
尽管坐在轮椅上，仍然爱咆哮，
相信自己的每句话都是真理，
相信他远在异国的公寓房
有一天仍然会成为作战指挥部，
而更多的人厌倦了在芦苇荡里
不停地躲避缉私船那强烈光束的射击，
他们想要回到大街上，回到
褪色的地图上重点一盏日常的灯，
他们回来了，在一把旧伞中
撑开童年的天空，在深夜的广场上
候鸟般啜吸记忆的水洼……
哦，缺席得太久，而舞台
已经旋转到另一边，就像冷漠的车流
悬置起天桥上的卖艺人，当
你的眼神因为没有人能从你的脸上
记起昔日的世界而变得阴郁，
当你的指控不过是喃喃自语，伴随着
空旷的楼道中某处水管的滴答声，
当敌人在时光中变得隐形，
难以从正面再遭遇——
你必须忍受遗忘如同退休者
坐在公园的长椅上凝视枯叶的飞旋，
当梦想的奖章迟迟不颁发，
当荣誉的纪念碑注定在你生前建不成，
哦，先驱，别变节在永恒之前最后的几秒。

The Pioneer

One among them,
though in a wheelchair, still loves ranting
and believes every sentence he speaks is true,
believes that his apartment, faraway in a foreign land
would one day turn into a combat headquarters,
while more people are tired of hiding
in reed beds from the searchlights on a patrol boat.
They want to go back onto the streets, to go back
to rekindle the lamp of everyday life on faded maps.
They have returned and opened a childhood sky
in an old umbrella, sipping puddles of memory
like migrant birds on the night square…
ah, the absence lasted too long, and the stage
already moved on, like indifferent traffic
leaving a busker stranded on the overpass.
Your gaze turns moody for there is no one
who can remember the bygone world from your face.
When your accusations are mere mutterings
in chorus with the dripping pipes in some empty hallway,
when enemies become invisible with time,
impossible to encounter face to face—
you must stand this forgetting like a retiree
sitting on the park bench watching the swirl of dry leaves.
When the dream medal has yet to be awarded,
when the memorial plaque will not be completed before your death,
ah, dear pioneer, do not recant in the last seconds before eternity.

隐形人

　—悼张枣

I

一个延长的冬天，
雪在三月仍然飘落，枝头
没有叶子但候鸟们如期归来，
履行了一场伟大的穿越；在图宾根，
你的出发地，卸下了翅膀的你
被卷进死亡的床单，永不再飞还。

很久以前你就是一个隐形人，
诗代替你翱翔，投影在我们中间，
被追踪，被传诵；早于
那狂欢的年代被坦克的履带碾成碎末，
也早于我踉跄地写下第一行诗，你
就已远走他乡。黑森林边一座偏僻的巢穴，

航摄图上蠕动的小黑点，匿名的漂流物；
那里，经历了航线最初的震撼，
你像通红的烙铁掉进冬日的奈卡河……
随一阵嘶响消散在涟漪的，不止是
那团貔貅般挥舞禁锢之爪的浓烟，还有
沸腾的青春，遍野为美充血的耳朵——

琴弦得不到友谊的调校、家园的回声，
演奏，就是一个招魂的动作，
焦灼如走出冥府的俄耳甫斯，不能确证
在他背后真爱是否紧紧跟随？那里，
自由的救济金无法兑换每天的面包，
假释的大门外，兀立K和他的成排城堡。

The Invisible Man

—An Elegy for Zhang Zao

I

An extended winter,
snow was still falling in March, no leaves were
on the branches and yet migrant birds returned in time,
completing their great expedition; in Tübingen,
your place of departure, you laid down your wings,
tangled into shrouds, and flew no more.

For a long time you had been an invisible man,
poetry did the flying for you, casting shadows among us,
their traces followed, their lines recited; before
tank treads crushed the carnival age to pieces,
before I staggered to write the first line, you departed.
An isolated nest by the edge of the Black Forest,

a black dot wriggling on the aerial map, anonymous flotsam;
there you experienced the first shocks on the journey,
like a hot, red iron you fell into the Neckar river in winter…
after the sizzling dispersed in the ripples, not only were there
delusional fumes with life-denying claws, but also riled youth
and ears everywhere, swelled with blood at the sight of beauty—

strings not tuned by friendship or echoes of home,
plucking is a gesture to beckon ghosts,
seething like Orpheus from the netherworld, unsure
whether true love followed close behind. There,
alms of freedom could not be cashed in for bread,
outside the probation door, a lonesome K and his rolls of castles.

哦，双重虚空的测绘员；往往
静雪覆夜，你和窗玻璃上的自己对饮，
求醉之躯像一架渐渐瘫软的天平，
倦于再称量每一个词语的轻重，
任凭了它们羽翎般飘零，隐没在
里希滕斯坦山打字机吐出的宽如地平线的白纸。

II

我第一次见你是在上海。在
逼仄的电梯间你发胖的身体更显臃肿，
全无传闻中的美男子踪影，然后，
在酒吧里你卖弄一种纸牌的小魔术，
好像它能够为你赎回形像的神奇——
我惊讶于你的孩子气，膨胀的甜蜜，

但有一个坚硬的核；我惊讶于
你入睡后如同渣土车般吵醒着街道的
鼾声，它如同你说过的"坏韵"，
困难地转换在你呼吸的两种空气——
与其说德语是冰，汉语是炭，不如说
现在是冰，过去是炭，相煎于你的肺腑。

中国在变！我们全都在惨烈的迁徙中
视回忆为退化，视怀旧为绝症，
我们蜥蜴般仓促地爬行，恐惧着掉队，
只为所过之处尽皆裂为深渊……而
你敛翅于欧洲那静滞的屋檐，梦着
万古愁，错失了这部离乱的史诗。

Ah, the surveyor doubled over in boredom; often quiet snow
blanketed night as you drank to yourself in the window pane,
body desirous of inebriation like a slowly sagging scale,
tired of weighing every word,
letting them flutter and then lie buried on the horizon
of white papers spit from Mr. Lichtenstein's typewriter.

II

I first saw you in Shanghai. In a cramped elevator
your pudgy physique was more corpulent than ever,
not a sign of the handsome youth of hearsay.
Then at a bar, you showed off a card trick,
as if it would redeem your miraculous image—
I was taken aback by your boyishness, your bloated sweetness,

yet you were tough at your core; I was taken aback
by your snoring, loud as a dump truck
waking up the streets, like the "bad rhymes" you mentioned,
shifting strenuously in the two airs that you breathed—
rather than saying German is ice, Chinese the ember, why not
say the present is ice, the past is ember, sizzling inside of you.

China is changing! We are all in the throes of migration.
Seeing remembrance as regression, nostalgia as a terminal disease,
we scuttle like lizards, afraid of lagging behind,
but everything we pass cracks into an abyss…
you folded your wings under the static eaves of Europe, dreaming
of timeless grief, missing the current epic of displacement.

你归来，像夜巡时走错了纬度的更夫，
像白日梦里的狄奥根尼，打着灯笼，
苦苦地寻觅……空气中不再有
言说的芬芳，钟子期们的听力已经涣散，
欢笑如多年前荒郊燃放的一场烟火；
只有你固执地铺展上一个年代的地图，

直到闪现的匕首让你成为自己的刺客，
心碎于乌有，于是归来变成了再次隐形，
落脚于一根教鞭，一张酒桌，
一座自造的文字狱；宁愿失声，
在喧哗的背面崩断琴弦，
不愿盘桓修辞的政坛，饶舌的舞台。

今夜，抽取书架上你那薄薄的一册，
掩卷后看见一颗彗星拖拽开屏的尾巴，
下方，两座大陆的笼子敞开——
一如诗人惯来是死后的神话，
类人猿中的鸟科，无地的君王；
或许你从来就没有真正地着陆。

You returned, like a watchman patrolling the wrong latitude,
like Diogenes of Sinope daydreaming with a lantern in hand,
searching tirelessly… there were no longer fragrant discourses
in the air, the likes of Zhong Ziqi were going deaf,
laughter like fireworks set off on the bleak outskirts many years ago;
only you spread out the map of the last age, stubbornly,

until a dagger's flash made you your own assassin.
Heart in pieces, you returned to a new invisibility,
and were reduced to a teacher's ruler, to a barroom table,
to your homemade prison of words; preferring to lose voice,
behind the clamor, your strings were snapped, no more lingering
in rhetoric's political arena, on a rapper's stage.

Tonight, I pull your slim volume from the shelf.
After closing the book, I see a comet with its tail trailing behind it.
Down below, the cages of two continents open up—
just as poets are myths after death,
birds among apes, kings of no land;
perhaps you never truly landed on earth.

Note: In a Chinese legend, Zhong Ziqi is a woodcutter who truly understands the music
of the Chinese Zither player Yu Boya. After Ziqi's death, Boya smashes his Zither and
plays no more. This legend exemplifies the Chinese ideal of friendship.

蝴蝶泉

这地名在一首流传甚广的民歌里出现过。有一年夏天,我在昆明一位女士的陪伴下,怀着对蝴蝶的想像和热情,沿那里的山径而行。巨大的榕树,幽清的泉流,但没有发现蝴蝶;直到我们穿越一大片人工整饰过的风景区,才看见那种小小的、白色的粉蝶在草坪上翻飞,它们是蝴蝶的家族里最寻常的一类,不过,也很迷人。

蝴蝶们都跑到哪里去了?后来,我们走进了一座昏暗的、恍然已多年无人光顾的蝴蝶博物馆里,那里的墙上挂满了蝴蝶,种类有数十种,数量却有几万只甚至更多,每一种类都被不厌其烦地重复,好像罐头里的沙丁鱼密密麻麻地排列,好像土豆堆积着。我们感到气闷,逃跑般地离开了。

山坡上,当地人向我们兜售着他们自己制作的、镶好了镜框的标本,其中有一些罕见的品种,是从海拔更高的山林中捕捉到的。我们跟随其中一位来到某座工场,那是一家废弃的工厂库房所在。他的合伙人正在空旷的房子里制作标本,膝盖上摊放着一堆东西,针筒、剪子、镊子、刷子和别的什么,空气里充满了福尔马林的气味,我的眼睛被刺激得流出了泪水。我们绕到这房子的背后去,那是一大块水门汀空地,地上摊放着无数张旧报纸,每张报纸上都挤满了死去的蝴蝶,它们体内的液质已被抽空,经过防腐处理后,放在这里等待晾干。

四周沉寂之极,空气中没有任何会动的东西,绿色的山体似乎在恐怖中凝固,在我的一生中从来没有见过这么多的蝴蝶,然而,这恰好也意味着我从来也没有见过这么多的尸体。

Butterfly Spring

We had heard the name of this place in a widely popular folk song. One summer, harboring enthusiastic visions of butterflies, a young lady from Kunming accompanied me up the mountain trail. Giant banyans, clear springs, but no butterflies; not until we crossed a manmade park did we see small white butterflies flutter over the lawn. They were the most average type in the butterfly family, but charming nonetheless.

Where had the butterflies gone? Then we walked into a dim butterfly museum, barely visited for years. Butterflies were mounted everywhere on the walls—a few dozen species of them—but in a quantity that must have reached the tens of thousands. Each variety was relentlessly repeated, arranged in close rows like canned sardines, heaped like potatoes. We felt short of breath and made a dash for the exit.

On the descent, the locals tried to sell us their homemade framed specimens, including some rare ones caught in higher-altitude forests. We followed one of the sellers to his workspace, which turned out to be set up at an unused factory warehouse. His partners were in the vast interior, working on specimens. Laid out on their laps were pincushions, scissors, tweezers, brushes, and other such objects. The air was so filled with formalin that my eyes teared up. We went around to an open sandy area at the back of the building. Great numbers of old newspapers were laid out on the ground, each sheet crowded with dead butterflies; their bodily fluids had been extracted and after treatment with preservatives they had been set out to dry in the sun.

All around was deep silence; nothing moved in the still air. The green hulk of the mountain seemed to have solidified in terror. I had never seen so many butterflies in my life—this also meant that I had never seen so many corpses.

好天气

天气好极了，
绿色的欢呼从张开的树枝间涌出，
在天空变成了蓝缎带和白云；
清洁工打扫着马路，
冬青丛中的鸟儿，羽毛比彩绘邮票还鲜艳。
每件事物都是它们应该是的样子，
清晰，夺目，闪动着光亮的尊严，
甚至大楼侧面的一道污渍，
甚至围拢在垃圾袋口的苍蝇……
仿佛都来自永恒的笔触。天气
好极了，这就像东欧的那些小国
从极权中醒来的第二天早晨，
长夜已经过去，不再有宵禁，
不再有逃亡，不再有镇压……
日子像摇篮，像秋千，在乡间小院的
浓荫下发出甜蜜的召唤；远方，
流亡者想要回家，就像约会的路上
歌在喉头发痒。可是，阴郁如
马内阿，踌躇于归与不归之间，
他预感到自己的所见将比往日更惊心……
是的，还会有坏天气，还会有
漫长的危机，漫长的破坏；痛苦
很少有人愿意继承，将它转化为财富。
恶，变得更狡诈，无形的战争才刚刚开始，
焚毁的旗帜依然飘扬在思想中，行动中，
胜利者自己却浑然不觉……
至于我们，尚且在时差格栅的远端排队，
就像蜗牛背负着重壳并且擎住一根天线般的触角，
我们只不过是好天气的观光客，触角
偶尔会伸出大气层的窟窿。

Fine Weather

Terrific weather,
green cheers surge forth from among spreading branches,
the sky turns into white clouds and blue ribbons;
cleaners sweep streets, birds perch in winterberry bushes
whose feathers are more brilliant than colored stamps.
Everything is the way it should be,
clear, striking, pulsating with brilliant dignity,
even the stain on the side of the building,
even the flies swarming around the mouths of trash bags...
as if it all comes from the brush stroke of eternity. The weather
terrific, like the morning when small Eastern European countries
awaken from despotism,
the long night over, no more curfew,
no more fleeing, no more repression...
like a cradle, like a swing, beneath the shade
of a country courtyard, days call out sweetly; from afar,
refugees want to return home, like a song stuck in the throat,
itching on the way to a date. Yet melancholic like
Norman Manea over whether to return or not,
he foresees sights more shocking than what he saw in the past...
yes, there will be bad weather, there will be
long crises, enduring damage; suffering
few are willing to inherit and turn into wealth.
Evil more cunning than ever, invisible wars have just started,
charred flags still fly in the head, in the act,
only the victors know not what they do...
as for us, we still line up behind metal bars that lead to jetlag.
Like snails carrying heavy shells and stretching out antennae,
we are nothing but witnesses of fine weather, antennae
occasionally poking holes in the atmosphere.

Note: Norman Manea is a Romanian writer who has lived in the U.S. since 1989.

圣索沃诺岛小夜曲

六月是一道永远会发炎的伤口，
即使远在威尼斯，我也能
嗅到那份暴力的腥臭
尾随着海风涌来；在记忆的禁忌中
沉默得太久，我们已经变成
自我监禁的铁门上咬紧铜环的兽首——

这里，环行的碧波
一遍遍冲刷我们心底的暗礁
和舌苔上的锈；对岸，军械库
静静地陈列艺术品，刚朵拉
像一架架秋千满载甜蜜的梦境，
从昼摆向夜，从夜摆到昼。

圣马可广场以一只悦耳的水罐
不断地往杯中倾倒歌声，夜深后
仍然有小酒吧像塞壬的裙摺间
滚落的珍珠，让旅客动心于捡拾……
水的藤条和光的锻带编扎的摇篮城，
晃动着，哼唱着，溶解着乡愁。

迷失在深巷中我嗅出一个不忠的自己，
想要就此隐遁到某扇窗的背后……
当火山已沉寂，空气中不再有怒吼，
难道阳台上的一盆花，客厅里的扶手椅，
天光板上波光造就的湿壁画，
不就是我们还能拥有的全部的家？

San Servolo Nocturne

June is a forever-inflamed wound.
Even in Venice, I can still smell
the stinking odor of violence tagging
along with the sea wind; in the forbidden grounds of memory,
silent for too long, we become the animal heads
that bite at bronze knobs on the door of self-incarceration—

here, curving azure waves
beat again and again against the shoals of our hearts
and the rust on our tongue; on the other shore, the armory
quietly displays artwork, like swings freighted
with honey in a dream the gondolas
rock from day toward night, from night toward day.

Piazza San Marco pours songs into cups
from a water jug pleasant to the ears. Once night deepens
there are still small pubs like pearls that roll
from the folds of a siren's dress, luring tourists to retrieve them…
water's cane and light's ribbon weave a cradle of the city,
swinging, humming, melting away the longing for home.

Lost in the deep alleys I smell an unfaithful self,
which seeks to shelter itself behind some window…
when the volcano falls silent and the air no longer soars,
what more than a flower plant on the balcony, an armchair
in the living room and a Buon Fresco of wavy light on the ceiling
could we claim as our home?

告诉我，经历了重创之后
揉皱的心能否重新舒展为帆？
为什么我醉倒在海天一色之中，眼眶里
却滚动着一场未完成的哭泣？
头枕层迭的涛声，大教堂的尖顶
就像一座风中的烛台伴我守灵到天明。

Tell me, can the corrugated heart unfold
to sail after a great blow?
Why am I drunk on the monochrome of sea and sky,
while my eyes still brim with unfinished crying?
Pillowed on the layers of the sea, like a candelabra
the cathedral dome keeps vigil with me until dawn.

小镇，1984

那些日子比现在真实。
晚饭之后，电影院像一盏煤油灯
捻亮在空荡如桌面的小镇上，
讲故事的祖父已经去世，
和我们的童年一起埋在了乡村；
我们将手插在裤兜里寻找新的快乐，
溜冰，看电影，游荡在老街上，
用口哨吹奏着一支《流浪者之歌》。

那些日子里微风掀动旧屋顶
就像要吹掉退伍老兵的黄军帽，
他肋骨处的伤疤与贫穷一样
不再可炫耀。父母们脸上的阴霾
被春光冲淡，可他们仍然习惯
低低地说话，虔诚地读报。
而我们在课堂上打盹，或者偷看
抽屉里摊开的杂志，传抄流行歌词。

夏天的火烧云点燃河流，荒丘
和槐树上的枯藤；稻田的蛙鸣
深夜闯过薄墙来和我们梦里的未来
激烈地争吵。那老得已经将眼睛
藏进皱纹里的老太太踩高跷般
到裁缝铺监制她的寿衣，桂花
开了又落，过路大卡车在风中
留下的汽油味，比任何气息更醉心。

Small Town, 1984

Those days were realer than these days.
After supper, the cinema was like a kerosene lamp
turned up bright in this small town as empty as the tabletop.
The storytelling grandfather was gone,
buried in the countryside along with our childhood;
we put our hands in our pockets to find happiness,
we skateboarded, watched films, wandered the old streets,
and whistled "Song of a Gypsy."

Those days light winds upturned old roofs
as if blowing off a veteran's khaki cap.
His scars on the ribs, like poverty, could no longer
show off. Gloomy weather on our parents' faces
was tempered by spring light, but they still had the habit
of talking softly, reading papers piously.
We dozed off in the classroom or sneaked a peek
at magazines in a drawer and copied out the lyrics of pop songs.

The volcanic clouds of summer lit up rivers, bare hills
and dry vines on locust trees; frog songs from the paddies
broke through thin walls at night and argued heatedly
with the future in our dreams. As if walking on stilts,
the old lady, so old that her eyes shrank into wrinkles,
ordered a shroud for herself at the tailor's. Osmanthus flowers
opened and fell. Passing trucks left gas fumes
more enchanting than any other smell on the wind.

老镜框里，披衣坐在贝加尔湖边的
列宁读什么？我读墙上的污渍，
武侠书，《天方夜谭》和俄罗斯小说
（怎么也记不住那些人物拗口的姓氏）；
没有秘密读物，这里寒冬比城市更漫长——
即将为我热爱的诗歌，或许早已经写出，
或许正在诞生，它们就像星光
穿越大气层，还要过一些日子才到达。

In the old picture frame, what was Lenin reading under a coat
on Lake Baikal? I read the stain on the wall,
kung fu stories, Arabian Nights, and Russian novels
(I could never remember the characters' tongue-twisting names);
no secret reading matters, cold winter here ran longer than in
    the city—
the poetry that I was about to love had perhaps been written
    already,
was perhaps being born, like starlight passing
through the atmosphere, a few days before its arrival.

故事
　—献给我的祖父

I

老了，老如一条反扣在岸上的船，
船舱中蓄满风浪的回声；
老如这条街上最老的房屋，
窗户里一片无人能窥透的黑暗。

大部分时光他沉睡在破藤椅上，
鼾声就像厨房里拉个不停的风箱，
偶尔你看见他困难地抬起手臂，
试图驱赶一只粘在鼻尖上的苍蝇。

但是当夜晚来临，煤油灯
被捻亮在灰黑的玻璃罩深处，
他那份苍老就变成了从磨刀石上
冲走的、带铁锈味的污水——

II

他开始为我们讲故事了。
沙哑的嗓音就像涨潮的大河，
越过哮喘症的暗礁和废弃的码头，
越过雾中的峡谷直奔古代的疆场。

沿途有紧握耕犁的勇士，即使
在睡梦中也圆睁双眼，听见潮起
如同听见号角的长鸣，立即
就投入到一场永恒的搏斗。

Stories

—To My Grandfather

I

Old, old like a boat facedown on the shore,
as cargo it held the echoes of stormy waves;
old like the oldest house on this street,
an impenetrable darkness flashed through the window.

Mostly he slumbered on a brittle wicker chair,
his snore ceaselessly pumping bellows in the kitchen.
Now and then you would see him raise a heavy arm
to shoo a fly that clung to the tip of his nose.

When night fell, the kerosene lamp
was turned up bright, deep in its sooty glass top,
his aged frailty would drain away
like water scented with a whetstone's rust—

II

Then he would start telling us stories.
His hoarse voice was like the flood tide of a river
that passed shoals of asthma and abandoned docks
through fogbound gorges into ancient battlefields.

Along the way staunch men gripped tight to plows,
their eyes glaring even in dreams. Hearing the rising tide
as if hearing the bugle call, they immediately
threw themselves into another endless fight.

刀剑的每次相交和战马的每次嘶叫，
注定在我的脑海里激起骇浪，
而低垂于秋风的帐篷里，
女人眼中的溪流，濡湿我的脸。

III

那些比他还要年老的故事，
那些他很小的时候从很老的人
那里听来的故事，以及
每次远行中寻觅到的故事，就是

他赤贫的一生攒下的全部金币，
存放在他的大脑中，
从没有弄丢过，在每个夜晚
都会发出悦耳的碰撞。

IV

如今他已经长眠于地下，
盛殓他骨灰的那只黑胡桃木盒子
已经像一只收音机连同电波
消逝在泥土的深处。如今

那些故事裹上一层硬封套，
就像标本，完整而精美，排列在书架上；
我偶然地逗留，吹掸去灰尘，
在其中默默地浏览，寻觅，

但是我深知，不再有
真正的故事和讲故事的人了，
夜晚如此漫长，空如填不满的深渊，
熄灯之后，心中也不再升起亮若晨星的悬念。

Each clash of swords and neigh of battle steeds
would stir roaring waves of dread in my mind,
and within a tent that leaned in the autumn wind,
a stream in a woman's eyes wet my cheek.

III

Stories older than him,
those stories that he heard when very young
from the very old, and stories
brought back from faraway journeys, these were

all the gold coins that he laid by in a life
of poverty, saved up in the vault of his mind,
never misplaced, and every night
their jingling made a delightful sound.

IV

Now he sleeps long under the earth.
Like a radio with its waves,
the black walnut box that holds his ashes
has vanished in the deep of the earth, and now

the stories are wrapped in stiff bindings
like specimens, perfect and neat, lined up on shelves;
at times I linger, blow, or flick off settled dust,
and page through quietly, searching,

but I know all along, there will never again
be true stories nor their tellers.
Night so long, empty like an unfathomable abyss, after the lights
go out no more suspense rises in the heart, bright like a morning star.

喇叭

酷暑还未销尽，老槐树的叶子
卷刃在日光下；在母亲的臂弯里
我闭上眼睛，假装在沉睡，
手掌里悄悄转动着心爱的玻璃球——

我厌恶午睡这昏庸的家庭制度，
外边，知了在低俯的树枝上唱着歌，
蝌蚪在水中孵化，从田野的尽头
传来大轮船驶过运河时鸣响的汽笛。

突然，得救了！一阵嘶嘶的电流
蛇行于村庄那没入草丛的沉寂，大人们
惺忪着睡眼，脚底拖动着无形的镣铐，
从屋中走出，聚到了那根电线杆下，

强光刺目，大喇叭高高地悬挂
就像电影里岗楼哨卫发亮的头盔
在俯瞰整座监狱，天空的湛蓝反衬着
一个停摆的刑期，男低音宣告领袖之死。

这消息像泥瓦匠的刮刀
瞬间抹平了所有人脸上的表情，然后，
伴随着哀乐声他们围成一面土墙，
低垂的头颈就像向日葵折断的茎秆。

而我狂喜于母亲的手不再将我搂紧，
玻璃球可以沿着泥泞欢快地蹦跳，
绕过水塘、稻草堆和打麦场，
一直滚动到村外的小树林——

The Loudspeaker

Scorching summer not yet over, old locust leaves
curled in sunlight; in mother's arms
I closed my eyes, faking sleep,
in my palms my beloved marbles rolled quietly—

I hated afternoon naps, this fatuous family ritual.
Out the door, cicadas sang on low branches,
tadpoles hatched in water, from the edge of the fields
whistles blasted as big ships passed through the canal.

Suddenly, saved! A sizzling electric current
snaked through the stillness that bided in the village bushes, adults
blinked open their sleepy eyes, dragged unseen shackles underfoot,
walked out of rooms, and gathered by the utility pole.

With a dazzling glare, a big loudspeaker hung high
like a warden's bright helmet on the watchtower in a film
that surveyed the whole prison, as the clear blue sky offset
a delayed execution and a baritone announced the leader's death.

This news, like a mason's trowel,
instantly scraped off every facial expression.
Then, to the tune of a dirge, they circled like an earthen wall,
their heads sagged like bent-over sunflower stems.

I was wild with joy that mother's hands clutched mine no more,
marbles could jump in joy along dirt roads,
around ponds, straw piles, and threshing floors of wheat,
and roll to the small forest outside the village—

这里，喇叭声之间交叉扫射的死角，
静得能听见鸟翅的扑动，低矮的灌木丛
骨节在发育的劈啪声，能听见旷野里
牛的哞鸣撕破灵堂般的死寂；透过

林边那窗栅般的枝条，我眺望
绵延的野草吞没了祖辈们的小路，
那弯垂中蜿蜒向天际的河流
如同空白的五线谱，等待着新的填写。

我并不知道从那时候开始，自己的脚步
已经悄悄迈向了成年之后的自我放逐，
迈向那注定要一生持续的流亡——为了
避免像人质，像幽灵，被重新召唤回喇叭下。

here, in a nook swept by the intersecting blare of the loudspeaker,
so quiet that fluttering wings and the cracking joints of spurting
    shrubs
were audible, the moos of cattle could also be heard
rending the funeral-parlor hush of fields, and through

lattice-like twigs in the forest, I watched
spreading wild grass devour the lanes of past generations,
bends of the river wind toward the horizon,
like empty staves, waiting to be refilled.

I did not know that from then on my steps
were tacitly turned toward the self-banishment of adult years,
toward this endless fated exile—to keep from being summoned
back under the loudspeaker, like a hostage, like a ghost.

IV (2012-)

佛罗伦萨

匆忙的一天。被迷路耽误了
行程。研究着地图而忘记
我们已经置身那些阴郁迷人的
街道和建筑，可以无知地漫游在
它突然被恢复的匿名状态。

或许这也是佛罗伦萨自身所渴望的，
否则它不会频繁地设定闭馆日
而将游客留在台阶上，广场上；
它用雄伟的大理石墙保护一种静穆，
在关闭的教堂内部，分泌空。

每个地方都可以对应某种人的形象，
佛罗伦萨让我想到一个老妇人，
她站在沉重的深紫色窗幔背后
向外看，嘴角挂着冷嘲，客厅里
挂着一小幅从未公开过的波提切利。

我戚然于这种自矜，每当外族人
赞美我们古代的艺术却不忘监督
今天的中国人只应写政治的诗——
在他们的想象中，除了流血
我们不配像从前的艺术家追随美，

也不配有日常的沉醉与抒情；
在道德剧烈的痉挛中，在历史
那无尽的褶皱里，隔绝了
一个生命对自己的触摸，沦为
苦难的注脚，非人的殖民地。

Florence

A day of rush. Itineraries delayed
by getting lost. We study the map and forget
we are already in those pensively charming
alleys and structures, roaming obliviously
through its newly recovered anonymity.

Perhaps this is what Florence longs for,
otherwise it would not close its churches so often,
leaving tourists on the steps and in the square;
with magnificent marble it walls off a somber quietude
in the interior of a closed church, secreting emptiness.

Every place corresponds to the image of a person.
Florence reminds me of an old lady, standing
behind thick violet curtains looking outward,
mouth tilted in irony, in whose living room
hangs a small privately-owned Botticelli.

I worry about her restraint. Whenever people
praise our ancient art yet insist that
the Chinese today should only write political poetry—
in their imagination, aside from the bloodshed,
we do not deserve to seek beauty like artists before us,

nor do we have the right to indulge in the mundane and song;
in sharp spasms of morality, in the endless folds
of history, a life's touch becomes
estranged from itself and is reduced
to footnotes about hardships and inhumane colonies.

所以我宁愿佛罗伦萨是敞亮的，
浅平的，如同露天咖啡馆的碟子，
那前来送甜点的女服务员因为意识到
我们注意着她的裙子而放缓了动作，
像一个蓬松的、熟透的贝阿德里采——

午后的阳光卸下了每棵树的重量，
叶子的毛细血管扩展于风，那些阴影
经过我们的额头时变成另一种逗留，
那些警卫在拱廊里自语：从任何
博物馆的窗口向外看，总是美丽的。

Thus I would prefer that Florence be brightly open,
flat and even, like a plate at an outdoor café.
That waitress who comes to serve our desserts,
slowing her steps as she notices us staring at her skirt,
looks like a fluffy-haired, overripe Beatrice—

afternoon sunlight unloads the weight of every tree,
the leaves' capillaries expand in the wind, and their shadows
pass over our foreheads and become another pause.
Guards talk to themselves in the arched hallways; peering
from every museum window, it is beautiful out and out.

古城

—赠洪磊

老如你的叔叔就可以解脱，
就可以端着茶壶躺在檐下的藤椅，
可以背负双手悠然地望天，
哼着小曲，踏着碎石板路而行。

而你始终有一种不满足，
从积下数年灰尘、如今
再次被拭净的这扇窗望出去，
你望见小城是一艘栓牢在缆桩上的船——

它周边的丘陵是彻底凝固了
起伏的波浪，它的码头
像工业的弃妇，输给了铁路。
它的人群是船身上幽深的青苔。

浪迹在遥远的大都市你厌倦
时针的疯转，利益的桅杆相互倾轧；
这里，你惊骇于日常的虚无，
晴空下尚未枯败的芭蕉无端的折裂。

未来折叠在《推背图》的某一页。
你唯一的消遣变成了
轻风绕面的午后
和几个徐娘相约于往事。

Ancient City

—For Hong Lei

Old enough to be carefree like your uncle,
to hold a teapot, lie on a rattan bench under the eaves,
leisurely watch the sky hands behind the back,
hum a little tune, tread along a rip-rap path.

Yet you are still unsatisfied,
looking out from a window once coated
with years of dust, now newly cleaned,
you see that this small city is a boat tied fast to the cleats—

the hills around it have completely solidified
the undulating waves, its docks,
like industry's abandoned wives, give way to railroads,
its people are shadowy mosses on the hull.

Roving in the far metropolis you are tired of the mad spinning
of clock hands and the masts of clashing interests; here,
you are amazed at the void of the quotidian, at the pointless
    breaking
of yet unwithered banana leaves under a clear sky.

The future folds in a prophetic page of *Tui Bei Tu*.
On afternoons of face-cooling breeze,
your only amusement has become
to rendezvous in halcyon times with ladies past their prime.

Note: *Tui Bei Tu* is a Chinese prophecy book from the Tang dynasty.

路过

昨夜并未喝酒，醒来
却带着宿醉——在旅馆
罩上蒸汽的镜子前，我怔忡地
倾听城区的车流。这里
我认识一位朋友，抛开了天赋
忙于捕捉廉价的赞美；一个
古典文学教授，爱自己的文字胜过
爱他人；一个音乐学院毕业的女孩，
丢失了爱情却爱上这个地方，
她有三份工作和少得可怜的睡眠，
——比这些更悲伤，是
几代人的激情转眼已耗尽，每个人
匆匆地走着，诅咒着，抱怨着，
冥冥中像无数把生锈的剑粘在一起——
这个平常的春日，他们当中有谁
能察觉我带有苛责的思念？
就让他们保持过去的时光中最好的的样子吧。
就让我路过而不拜访，继续孤单的旅程——
嗓子干渴，舌头被烙铁灼伤，
想说的话盘旋在昏沉的大脑里，如此难产，
为此需要年复一年地默祷，
反复地拥抱阵雨，风景，岔路。
我脆弱如树影，在路面的水洼里
感受着被车轮碾过的疼痛；
我冷，因为对面没有光，
人们相见时，都是捻暗的灯笼。

Passing By

Not a drop last night, yet I wake
feeling hungover—before a steamed mirror
at a hotel, in shock, I
listen to the city's river of traffic. Here
I have a friend, who has brushed his gifts aside
and scurried to capture cheap praises; a
Classics professor, who loves his own words more
than he does others; a girl, a music school graduate
who lost a love yet fell in love with this place,
has three jobs and precious little sleep
—even sadder, the passion drained away
from several generations in a flash, all of them
rushing ahead, cursing, complaining,
like countless rusty swords impelled to stick together—
a normal spring day, who amongst them
could discern my exacting wishes?
Let them keep the best face on the past.
Let me pass by without a visit and continue my journey—
throat dry, tongue scorched by soldering iron,
words swirl in my dazed mind, so slow to come,
thus the need to pray year after year, to repeatedly
embrace rain showers, landscapes, and forked roads.
Frail like tree shadow, in the puddles on the road
I feel the pain of being rolled over by wheels;
I am cold, because there is no light on the other side.
When people meet, lanterns are turned low.

月亮上的新泽西

—致L.Z.

这是你的树，河流，草地，
你的大房子，你的美国，
这是你在另一颗星球上的生活，
你放慢车速引我穿行在山麓间，
就像在宽银幕上播放私生活的记录片。

大客厅的墙头挂着印象派的复制品，
地板上堆满你女儿的玩具，
白天，当丈夫去了曼哈顿，
孩子去了幼儿园，街区里静得
只剩吸尘器和割草机的交谈，
你就在跑步机上，像那列玩具火车
在它的环形跑道上，一圈又一圈地旋转……

这里我惊讶于某种异化，
并非因为你已经改换国籍
或者成为了别人的妻子，我
惊讶于你的流浪这么快就到达了终点——
我们年轻时梦想的乐土
已经被简化成一座舒适的囚笼，
并且，在厚厚的丝绒软垫上，
只要谈论起中国，你的嘴角就泛起冷嘲的微笑。

New Jersey on the Moon

To L.Z.

This is your tree, river, lawn,
your big house, your America.
This is your life on another planet,
you slow down the car to lead me through the foothills,
like a documentary of private life on the big screen.

Prints by the Impressionists hang on the living room wall,
your daughter's toys piled high on the floor.
When your husband commutes to Manhattan during the day
and your child to kindergarten, the streets fall silent
except for conversations between vacuum and lawn mower.
On the treadmill, like a toy train
on its oval track, you go around and around…

here I am surprised by a sense of strangeness,
not that you have already changed your nationality
or become someone's wife. I am
surprised that your wanderings have so soon come to an end—
the happy land of our youthful dreams
already abbreviated into a comfortable cage,
and on the thick velvet couch,
once we speak of China, your mouth curls in a smirk.

我还悲哀于你错失了一场史诗般的变迁，
一个在现实中被颠倒的时间神话：
你在这里的每一年，
是我们在故乡度过的每一天。
傍晚，我回到皇后区的小旅馆里，
将外套搭在椅背上，眼前飘过
当年那个狂野的女孩，爱
自由胜过梅里美笔下的卡门，走在
游行的队列中，就像德拉克洛瓦画中的女神。

……记忆徒留风筝的线轴，
我知道我已经无法带你回家了，
甚至连祝福也显得多余。
无人赋予使命，深夜
我梦见自己一脚跨过太平洋，
重回烈火浓烟的疆场，
填放着弓弩，继续射杀那些毒太阳。

I am saddened that you have missed an epic change in time,
a myth of time upended amid reality;
every one of your years here
is a day that we have spent back home.
At twilight, I return to the hotel in Queens,
put my coat on the back of the chair. Before my eyes,
that wild girl floats by, loving
freedom more than Mérimée's Carmen, walking
among the marchers in a parade, like a goddess painted by Delacroix

…memory retains nothing but the kite's spool.
I know I can no longer take you home,
even blessings seem unnecessary.
No one to entrust a mission to, deep in the night,
I dream of myself one step over the Pacific,
returned to fire-bright, smoke-thick battlefields,
loading my crossbow and shooting down those toxic suns.

九月，马德里

I

岁月安稳，如一片铺展在
坡地间的橄榄林，没有
太高的楼，没有太多的灰尘
和太多突然发迹的邻居；
店铺的门懒散，半掩在深巷，
吉它声殷勤地伴奏冗长的午餐。
远征的颂歌横躺在书架上，
革命已经结束，国王还在，
屋脊上多出几排英雄的雕像。
嗜血的冲动氧化，转变成
周末时为斗牛和足球爆发的欢呼；
吻，在蓝天下在干燥的空气中
火星般四溅，在海绵般柔软的
大块草地上逐渐沉淀成鲜花。

Madrid, September

I

Days are placid, like an olive grove
spread over the slopes, not
too many high-rises, not too much dust
or too many nouveau-riche neighbors;
shop doors sluggish, cracked ajar in deep alleys,
guitar notes gallantly accompany a lengthy lunch.
The paean to an expedition lies flat on the bookshelf,
revolution already over, the king remains,
new metal heroes file along the roof lines.
Bloodthirsty impulses oxidize and turn into
explosive cheers for weekend bullfights and soccer;
kisses, in the dry air under a blue sky,
are flung about like sparks, settling slowly
into flowers on soft, spongy lawns.

II

伫候在火车站成簇的荫凉里，
我忽然厌倦了旅行而想要居留，
想要在一小间公寓里点亮
绿布罩的台灯，晾在阳台上的
衬衫，蒸发了燥狂症的因子；
走过的路全都成为苍穹中
一道乳白色的飞机尾烟；
善，终于可以一点一滴积攒，
在人群中兑换到起码的尊严……
让众多的往事越过大西洋前来找我吧，
我爱退潮的沙滩胜过爱现场。
纵然自责如逃兵，纵然悔疚
如嫁给老鳏夫之后的少女，但
回去，就是流放。

II

Waiting forever under a clump of shade at the railway station,
out of the blue I feel tired of traveling and want to stay,
want to turn on a lamp with a green shade
in a small apartment, hang a shirt to dry
on the balcony, let the bipolar genes evaporate;
all roads traveled turn into the milky trail of smoke
behind a plane in sky's azure vault;
kindness finally gathers drop by drop,
and is exchanged for a modicum of dignity in the crowd...
let things past cross the Atlantic to come find me,
I love the beach during ebb tide more than being on the scene.
Though blaming oneself for desertion, though chargrinned
like a young girl married to a geezer, yet to re-
turn, is to be exiled.

双城记

那些滑翔在广告牌前的海鸟
也许从来就没见过广袤的陆地，
除了海，短促的地平线上看不到
别的风景；那些摩天高楼惟有
相互映照，在自己的玻璃上
将对方画成一座座陡峭的山脉，
将夜晚的车流画成一条条繁忙的运河。

每天我从旋转门汇入人潮，沿
细雨的街道一路搜寻旧日的梦境，
可是，就像透过所有大都市的橱窗——
我看见一些女人的眼睛受迪奥的刺激
而在其它的品牌前失明，我看见
灯光熄灭后那弹药库般的内心压力
仍然堆积在写字楼的每张办公桌上。

惟有出租车司机收听的老情歌
和上环那繁体字招牌林立的旧店铺，
榫接了我脑海里的另一个香港，
一个少年白日梦中的香港——
那只是几盒翻录的磁带，
几本传阅中被翻烂的色情杂志
和烟雾弥漫的房子里放映的武侠片……

我们饥饿的感官曾经贪婪地
攫取从它走私而来的这些微量元素，
并且在黑暗中以幻想的焊锡
合成一座遥远的新世界——
漫长的禁锢过后，它的方言
时髦如穿越防线的口令，甚至
整个内陆都倾斜成一艘划向尖沙嘴的

The Tale of Two Cities

Gliding before the billboards, those seabirds
have perhaps never seen the vast continent,
except for the sea, there is no landscape to be seen
on the abrupt horizon; those high-rises
only reflect each other, depicting the others
on their own glass as one steep ridge after another,
depicting the nightly traffic as one busy canal after another.

Every day I merge with tides of people through a revolving door,
along drizzling streets in search of a dreamscape long gone,
yet, like through every cosmopolitan window—
I see some women, eyes aroused by Dior
and blinded by other brands. I see
after the lights go out, the ammunition dump of psychic pressure
still heaped on every desk in an office building.

Only the old torch songs played by taxi drivers and
the old shops with traditional characters along Sheung Wan
dovetail with another Hong Kong in my mind,
the Hong Kong of a youngster's daydream—
just a few recorded cassettes,
a few well-riffled girlie magazines
and kung fu movies in a smoke-filled house...

our starved senses once greedily absorbed
these smuggled micronutrients
and fantasy welding done in the dark
assembled a far-off new world—
after lengthy confinement, its dialect
became fashion, like a command crossing lines of defense
until the whole Mainland teetered toward becoming a craft

偷渡船——是的，我将
内心岩浆的第一阵喷发归之于香港，
我将男孩和少妇之间永恒的时差
归之于香港……这就是为什么
我从未来过却好像旧地重游，并且
恍惚在旅馆的旋转门中，不知道被推开的
是多年之前的未来还是多年之后的过去？

smuggling toward Tsim Sha Tsui—yes, I
attribute the first eruption of my inner lava to Hong Kong,
I assign the eternal jetlag between a boy and a woman
to Hong Kong…this is why
it feels like a trip down memory lane, though I've never been here,
giddy in the revolving door, I do not know if it opens
to the future many years ago or to the past many years away?

时光的支流

小女孩的忸怩漾动在鱼尾纹里，
深黑色的眼镜框加重了她的疑问语气：
你还记得我吗？如此的一次街头邂逅
将你拽回到青春期的夏日午后——
一间亲戚家的小阁楼，墙头悬挂着
嘉宝的头像，衣服和书堆得同样凌乱，
一张吱嘎作响的床，钢丝锈断了几根；
那时她每个周末都会来，赤裸的膝盖
悬在床边荡秋千，絮语，爱抚，
月光下散步，直到末班车将她带走——
她的身体是开启你成年的钥匙，
她的背是你抚摸过的最光滑的丝绸，
没有她当年的吻你或许早已渴死……
现在你的生活如同一条转过了岬角的河流，
航道变阔，裹挟更多的泥沙与船，
而阁楼早已被拆除，就连整个街区
也像一张蚂蚁窝的底片在曝光中销毁——
从这场邂逅里你撞见了当年那个毛茸茸的自己
和泛滥如签证官的权力：微笑，倾听，不署名……
望着她漫上面颊的红晕，你甚至
不无邪恶地想到耽误在浪漫小说里的肺炎

The Bayou of Time

A little girl's bashfulness shimmers through her crow's feet,
black eyeglass frames lend weight to her questioning tone:
Do you still remember me? Such an encounter on the street
drags you back to a teenage summer afternoon—
an attic at a relative's house, Garbo's headshot
hung on the wall, clothes and books in equal messes,
a creaking steel cot, a few springs rusted and snapped;
she came every weekend then, her naked knees
dangling by the cot's edge as if on a swing, whispers, caresses,
walks under moonlight, until the last bus took her away—
her body was a key to open your manhood,
her back the most smooth silk that you had ever touched,
without her kiss you might have died of thirst…
now your life seems like a river past the headlands,
canals widened, bearing silt and boats along,
and the attic has been taken down, even the whole block,
like a negative of an ant nest has been destroyed by exposure—
in this encounter you bump into your downy self and the over-
    whelming
power of a visa officer: smile, listening, no approval issued…
watching the blush diffuse on her face, you even think,
not without mischief, of pneumonia tarrying in a romantic novel.

地理教师

一只粘着胶带的旧地球仪
随着她的指尖慢慢转动，
她讲授维苏威火山和马里亚纳海沟，
低气压和热带雨林气候，冷暖锋

如何在太平洋上空交汇，云雨如何形成。
而她的身体向我们讲授另一种地理，
那才是我们最想知道的内容——
沿她毛衣的V字领入口，我们

想像自己是电影里匍匐前行的尖兵，
用一把老虎钳偷偷剪开电丝网，且
紧张于随时会亮起的探照灯，
直到下课铃如同警报声响起……

我们目送她的背影如同隔着窗玻璃
觑觎一本摊放在桌面的手抄本。
即使有厚外套和围巾严密的封堵，
我们仍能从衣褶里分辨出肉的扭摆。

童话不再能编织夜晚的梦，我们
像玻璃罐里的蝌蚪已经发育，想要游入大河——
在破船般反扣的小镇天空下，她就是
好望角，述说着落日，飞碟和时差。

Geography Teacher

A taped old globe
spins slowly by her fingertips,
she teaches Vesuvius and the Mariana Trench,
depression and tropical climate, how cold and warm fronts

merge above the Pacific, how rain and clouds form.
Yet her body teaches us another kind of geography,
that is what we really want to know—
along the opening of her V-neck sweater, we

imagine ourselves as the crawling commandoes in a film,
cutting electric fences with a pair of pliers, and
nervous that the searchlight will light up at any time,
until the recess bell rings like an alarm set off…

we watch her leave as if peeking through the window
at the open book of notes on her desk.
Even under her thick coat and the firm barrier of a scarf,
we still make out the flesh swaying beneath the folds of her clothing.

Fairytales can weave no more night dreams, we have grown up,
like tadpoles in a glass jar ready to swim into rivers—
under the small-town sky that resembles a broken, upended boat,
she is the Cape of Good Hope, explaining sunsets, UFOs and jetlag.

读《米格尔大街》

温柔、苦涩的小书，
沿它的字里行间就可以
逛回我少年时居住的小街
甚至连人物也很雷同，
伊莱亚斯当时就住在隔壁，
埃罗尔是我的同桌，至于
布莱克·沃兹沃斯，这你们
可想不到，我们中学的政治教师，
写有黑色的、卡夫夫式的短篇，
以化名发表，他劝我："一生
很漫长，先想办法离开这地方。"

每一个人物似乎都可以
在这条街上找到原型，
他们已被我深深地遗忘，
重逢，发生在别人的书中，
发生在翻译里，发生在异国他乡。
文学企图穷尽旅行，而
在所有的路线中我发展了
自我放逐，那么多不够，
还需要回来，一次次地回来——
确曾在某个春日或夏日的午后，
当一阵风吹动整条街的窗帘，
我看见过生活的全部色彩。

On Reading *Miguel Street*

A bitter, tender, small book,
between its lines I could wander
back to the street where I lived as a youth.
Even the characters are similar,
Elias lived next door then,
Errol was my desk mate, and as for
Blake Wordsworth—this, you cannot imagine—
was our middle school political science teacher,
who wrote Kafkaesque noir novellas and
published under a pen name, who tried to persuade me,
"You have your life ahead of you, first find a way to leave here."

Every character seems to
find its archetype on this street.
They are long forgotten by me.
Reunion happens in other people's books,
happens in translation, happens in a foreign land.
Literature essays to exhaust all travels, yet,
I need to return, again and again
to all the routes on which I have developed
my self-exile, which is far from enough—
once on a spring or summer afternoon, when a gust
of wind blew every curtain on the street,
I saw all the brilliance of this life.

读曼德施塔姆夫人回忆录

迟到的书。假如读得更早，
我瞳孔里的钨丝就会被引爆，声带
在黑暗中变得透明，押炼狱的韵。
总是有小个子的巨人，和善于倾听他的
女性，为耳福忍耐了别的：饥饿，
恐惧或自己的一生；总是有提早退场
而在过道发生的相遇，借个火，嘲弄，
一起大笑着走向年代的背面。当心，
你的火星溅到了我的裙子上。不，
那是在众人的默认里烧出个大窟窿。
还敢再往前走吗？哪里？是要我
回去再对着克里姆林宫放一枪吗？
不，亲爱的，要学会解脱你自己，
我已无法陪在你身边，我必须留下来，
做一个现实的幽灵，铸造回音。

On Reading Mrs. Mandelstam's Memoir

A belated book. If I'd read it earlier,
a filament in my pupils would have gone out, my vocal cords
turning transparent in the dark, rhyming with purgatory.
There is always a little giant with a thoughtful female listener,
bearing all else for the ear's felicity: hunger,
fear, and her own life; there are always encounters in hallways
when leaving early, to borrow a lighter, to mock
and laugh while marching to the other side of the era. Watch out,
your cinders have splashed onto my skirt. No,
that was the big hole burned in the screen of public consent.
Dare we walk further? Where? Do you want me
to shoot another bullet at the Kremlin?
No, my dear, learn to let yourself go,
I can on longer be in your company, I must stay,
and become reality's wraith, casting echoes.

我想起这是纳兰容若的城市

我想起这是纳兰容若的城市，
一个满族男人，汉语的神射手，
他离权力那么近，离爱情那么近，
但两者都不属于他——短促的一生
被大剧院豪华而凄清的包厢预订，
一旦他要越过围栏拥抱什么，
什么就失踪。哦，命定的旁观者，
罕见的男低音，数百年的沉寂需要他打破——
即便他远行到关山，也不是为了战斗，
而是为了将辽阔和苍凉
带回我们的诗歌。当他的笔尖
因为吮吸了夜晚的冰河而陷入停顿，
号角声中士兵们正从千万顶帐篷
吹灭灯盏。在灵魂那无尽的三更天，
任何地方都不是故乡。活着，仅仅是
一个醒着的梦。在寻常岁月的京城，
成排的琉璃瓦黯淡于煤灰，
旗杆被来自海上的风阵阵摇撼；
他宅邸的门对着潭水，墙内
珍藏一座江南的庭院，檐头的雨
带烟，垂下飘闪的珠帘，映现
这个字与字之间入定的僧侣，
这个从圆月开始一生的人，
永远在追问最初的、动人的一瞥。

It Comes to Me That This Is Nalan Xingde's City

It comes to me that this is Nalan Xingde's city.
A Manchu man, a sharpshooter of the Chinese language,
he was so close to power, so close to love,
yet neither belonged to him—this short life
was reserved for the opulent and lonely boxes of opera houses.
When he wanted to cross the railings and embrace something,
it would disappear. Ah, fated witness,
rare baritone, only he could break centuries of silence—
even his journeys to border passes were not to fight battles,
but to bring back vastness and desolation
to poetry. When his brush tip
fell silent from soaking in the night's icy rivers,
soldiers in a myriad of tents were snuffing out lamps
while the bugle called. For the endless third watch of the soul,
nowhere was home. Living, merely for the sake
of a waking dream. In uneventful years in the capital,
rows of glazed roof tiles faded in soot, flagstaffs shook
in sea winds; the door to his mansion faced
a pond, inside the walls he treasured a courtyard
from South-of-Yangtze, rain from the eaves was wreathed
in smoke, gleaming bead curtains swayed to reveal
a monk, sitting quiet between words,
a man whose life began at a full moon,
always questing for that first moving glance.

Note: Nalan Xingde was a Qing dynasty poet.

TRANSLATOR'S NOTE
DONG LI

I first came to know Zhu Zhu's voice on a New England winter day over a trans-Pacific phone call that lasted a whole night. I wanted to translate his poems and needed permission. As the tone of his voice shifted from distanced skepticism to understated enthusiasm, we felt the trust and it dawned on us that this trust could be extended to a book. That's how everything started and our friendship began.

I kept thinking of his soft and resolute voice as I gathered his books and plunged deeper into winter and into his world.

Long, long winter,
a wolf looks for the forest of words.

These two lines seem to encapsulate Zhu Zhu the poet: a lone wolf utterly on the periphery with his treasured independence, as well as his unrelenting respect and unstoppable reach for words and their histories. As I selected poems from his robust twenty-five years of poetic output into one slim volume, I was looking at his "forest of words" that slowly both grew on me and accrued meaning with each reading.

As the long winter slowly melted into spring blossoms, as the trajectory of Zhu Zhu's poetic arc became clearer before my eyes, I was about to match the face to his familiar voice. I met him for the first time when he came to the United States for a joint-residency at the Vermont Studio Center. With an almost reticent demeanor, he quietly blended in. I remember at meals he always wanted to take a seat by the window, where the Gihon River could be heard. I often traced a trail of cigarette butts to find him sitting on the porch or by the Gihon, wreathed in smoke. I never saw him scribble down his impressions of the country or the residency, but toward the end of our time together, a stack of loose pages was slipped under my door. It smelled of burning.

After China's political upheaval in recent eras and the continuous capitalist frenzy, the "warm, languid routine" of a foreign writing residency did not seem to suit Zhu Zhu, as I often found him spinning and smashing at the Ping-Pong table or in one of the two bars in the village drinking away with the locals, communicating through his gestures and smiles. Over time his outlook has become more international, but he returns again and again to classical tales and historical figures, "brim[ming] with unfinished crying," and investigates their relevance to our times. His narrated and narrative histories are not "dressed as literary allusion / blending allure with parable," but are meant to be "a scalpel-like nib, to open / old China's chest." Even his more politically charged poems are not meant to take sides but to reflect a layered and nuanced aesthetic reading of history and politics. The poems remain open and resist easily reductive interpretations.

not become a ghost, not traffic in suffering,

but clarify life's wellspring—

Not to serve as a loudspeaker for a certain ideology, not to exorcise for sensational effects, Zhu Zhu excavates "the forbidden grounds of memory" by clarifying the ambivalence that a simple political reading might elide. He demands that poetry return to its ancient roots, where words first emerge and find their calling in fragments and lifelines.

Here is a fearlessly independent poet who maintains his cool and observes the world with his whole eyes as the political horizon blurs and shifts. What matters to him is how words silently explode and become explosives, and how language sinks and rises. Here is a poet who advocates poetry as "a pass for the despicable and the noble," an open field where everyone is welcome to speak up and sing. Here is a poet who reinvents himself from an early ethereal verse limned by the unspeakable, to a visual and visceral composition of images that impart the transient and untranslatable, to restrained and rich narrative investigations of historical figures and phenomena. Here is a poet who looks again to "the mundane and song," where the lyric finds its first note. This can seem like an indulgence in our profit-reigning attention-splintering age. Yet it is indeed in this indulgence that "sharp spasms of morality" and "endless folds of history" become music, memorable, and memory. It is indeed in this indulgence of poets roaming in word and world, of slow lines shuttling through the problems and prospects of the political, the historical, and the quotidian that poetry resists being reduced to footnotes and instead commands to be read and reread for what it illuminates.

> ...sitting quiet between words,
> a man whose life began at a full moon,
> always questing for that first moving glance.

It is winter again as I write this note. Our spring retreat in the Vermont country was years ago. As I go through the last proof of *The Wild Great Wall* in one long breath, these final smoked lines come alive again in Zhu Zhu's attentive voice. I lament the irretrievable loss of these Chinese words, whose constellation first moved me and sent me on a mission to look for the English words that could approximate the sensory traces and emotional pulls of the original. I feel consoled that the reader can now experience Zhu Zhu in the English language for the first time. As I shift between Zhu Zhu's Chinese and my English, our shared words, like trees in a forest, seem to grow with each season. Here is a lyric that continues to extend.

ACKNOWLEDGEMENTS

Many thanks to the editors and readers of the magazines in which these translations or their earlier versions first appeared:

Asia Literary Review: "Island in the Sea," "The Creeper"
Asymptote: "Florence," "On Reading Mrs. Mandelstam's Memoir,"
    "Ancient City," "The Tale of Two Cities" with Translator's Note
The Brooklyn Rail: "Clearing in the Woods," "Blue Smoke,"
    "The Wild Great Wall," "Small Town" with Translator's Note
Circumference, Poetry in Translation: "New Jersey on the Moon,"
    "Passing By"
EuropeNow, a Journal of Research & Art: "San Servolo Nocturne,"
    "Madrid, September," "On Reading *Miguel Street*"
Hayden's Ferry Review: "The Pioneer," "Butterfly Spring"
Lana Turner, a Journal of Poetry and Opinion: "Up the Stairs," "I am
    François Villon," "Duolun Road"
The Literary Review: "Small Town, 1984," "The Loudspeaker"
The Margins: "Stories"
Michigan Quarterly Review: "Inland," "It Comes to Me That This Is
    Nalan Xingde's City"
Nashville Review: "The Bayou of Time," "Geography Teacher"
North American Review: "Fine Weather"
Plume: "Small Town Saxophone," "The Kitchen Song"
Silk Road Review: "South-of-Yangtze, a Republic"
Tupelo Quarterly: "The Grotto," "To the North," "The Invisible Man"
Two Lines: "The Beach," "Days With a Swedish Friend," "Cold Front"
World Literature Today: "Old Shanghai"

"The Wild Great Wall," "The Creeper," "To the North," "Fine
Weather," "Florence," "New Jersey on the Moon," "On Reading
Mrs. Mandelstam's Memoir," "It Comes to Me That This Is Nalan
Xingde's City" were reprinted in *Poetry International*, 2017.

"Old Shanghai," "Clearing in the Woods," "Blue Smoke," "The Wild Great Wall," "Small Town," "The Pioneer," "Butterfly Spring," "New Jersey on the Moon," "Passing By" were reprinted and featured in *National Translation Month*, 2017.

"Days With a Swedish Friend" was nominated by *Two Lines* for the Pushcart Prize.

My gratitude to Zhu Zhu, Denis Mair, Forrest Gander, Han Lifeng, Song Lin, Liu Ligan, Chicu Reddy, Chiyuma Elliott and to Vermont Studio Center for the sanctuary to translate.

BIOGRAPHIES

Zhu Zhu was born in Yangzhou, P.R. China. He is the author of numerous books of poetry, essays, and art criticism, including a bilingual French edition translated by Chantal Chen-Andro. He's the recipient of Henry Luce Foundation Chinese Poetry Fellowship at the Vermont Studio Center and the Chinese Contemporary Art Award for Critics, and has been a guest at the Rotterdam and Val-de-Marne International Poetry Festivals. He lives in Beijing.

Dong Li was born and raised in P.R. China. He is an English-language poet and translates from the Chinese, English, and German. He's the recipient of a PEN/Heim Translation Grant and fellowships from Alexander von Humboldt Foundation, Akademie Schloss Solitude, Ledig House Translation Lab, Henry Luce Foundation/Vermont Studio Center, Yaddo, and elsewhere.

Printed in the USA
CPSIA information can be obtained
at www.ICGtesting.com
JSHW082353140824
68134JS00020B/2057

9 781944 700690